D0325768

G.P. TAYLOR

Sin, Salvation & Shadowmancer

G.P. Taylor

Sin, Salvation & Shadowmancer

AS TOLD TO BOB SMIETANA

ZONDERVAN®

GRAND RAPIDS, MICHIGAN 49530 USA

ZONDERVAN.COM/
AUTHORTRACKER

ZONDERVAN®

G. P. Taylor
Copyright © 2006 by G. P. Taylor

The author hereby asserts his moral right to be identified as the author of this work.

Published in association with Caroline Sheldon Literary Agency.

Requests for information should be addressed to:
Zondervan, *Grand Rapids, Michigan 49530*

Library of Congress Cataloging-in-Publication Data

Taylor, G. P.
    G. P. Taylor : sin, salvation and Shadowmancer / G. P. Taylor,
as told to Bob Smietana.
        p.   cm.
    ISBN-13: 978-0-310-26739-3 (acid-free paper)
    ISBN-10: 0-310-26739-0 (acid-free paper)
    1. Taylor, G. P. 2. Novelists, English — 20th century — Biography.
I. Smietana, Bob, 1965– II. Title.
PR6070.A92Z46   2006
823'.92 — dc22

                                                              2006010204

This edition printed on acid-free paper.

All Scripture quotations, unless otherwise indicated, are taken from the *Holy Bible: New International Version®*. NIV®. Copyright © 1973, 1978, 1984 by International Bible Society. Used by permission of Zondervan. All rights reserved.

All rights reserved. No part of this publication may be reproduced, stored in a retrieval system, or transmitted in any form or by any means — electronic, mechanical, photocopy, recording, or any other — except for brief quotations in printed reviews, without the prior permission of the publisher.

Interior design by Beth Shagene

Printed in the United States of America

---

06 07 08 09 10 11 12 • 19 18 17 16 15 14 13 12 11 10 9 8 7 6 5 4 3 2 1

To the Taylor Family
founded 23 July 1983
1 Peter 4:13
– G. P.

For Kathy, Sophie, Eli and Marel
You mean the world to me
– Bob

CONTENTS

PROLOGUE

For the first time in thirty years, I was about to be expelled from school. Unlike the other times I had run afoul of school authorities – when I'd set my desk on fire or dangled one of my best friends by his heels out the third-storey window – this time I had no idea what I had done wrong.

It was early October 2005, and one hundred fourteen-year-olds were packed into the school auditorium in Cornwall where I was speaking. Over the past few years, I have given hundreds of these talks in schools and bookshops in Britain and America. I use the time to fire up the students' imaginations and get them thinking about reading and books, instead of spending their time like zombies in front of the television.

"Don't watch television all your life. Next to books, TV is a load of crap," I said. "Remember, watching TV is easy; it's for dweebs, and it rots your brain."

I continued on the theme. "You can make a story out of anything. You can even write a story about a bogey."

With that, the whole auditorium burst out in laughter, and I knew I had their attention. (By the way, there is a famous children's book called *Fungus, the Bogey Man*.)

"All right, let's try to write a story. What happens to the bogey in the story?"

One of the students yelled out, "It gets arms and teeth and chases you down the street." They kept yelling out suggestions, and we made up a story right then and there.

The talk continued for another fifteen minutes and seemed to be a great success. Then without warning, the doors at the front of the auditorium burst open and several teachers walked in.

"Right, children, return to your classrooms," one announced in a terse voice. She and several other teachers began herding the children from the room.

I thought she was telling them off because of the noise. "I'm sorry, they got a bit excited."

"It's not that," she said. "It's the fact that you used the word *crap*. You also used the words *bogey*, *fart* and *bum*."

With that, she turned on her heel and left me in the auditorium. My face turned beet red as I stood there. I've given this same talk a hundred times and never had a single complaint. One of the students ran up to me as she was leaving and said, "G. P., that was real" – by that, I think she meant "cool."

Bum, *bogey* and *fart* – is that all it takes to be expelled from school these days? I use them all in my book *Tersias*, as they were commonplace in the eighteenth century, when the story is set. These words were good enough for Shakespeare and Chaucer but a step too far for G. P. Taylor. And none of my offended teachers seemed even remotely upset when I'd asked the students how many of them hadn't read a book in the last six months and 60 percent put their hands up in reply.

After the abrupt dismissal, I waited in the auditorium, hoping someone from the school would come and explain what was going on. But after about ten minutes, there still was no sign of the school staff, so my publicist and I left the building. We had another engagement that day.

The following morning, a group of students at Blackwells bookstore in Bristol were roaring with laughter over the news that I'd been tossed out of school. At the end of the talk, a reporter from one of the national newspapers was waiting for me; the paper wanted to run a story about my being expelled in Cornwall. *They must be hard up for news*, I thought.

Just a few years ago, no one knew my name, but now it's worldwide news when I get tossed out of school. Never in a million years did I dream this was possible, when, in the autumn of 2002, I sold my motorcycle and self-published a book called *Shadowmancer*, a book that for one summer became "hotter than Potter" and changed my life. I was soon heralded as the new C. S. Lewis. My book became a *New York Times* number one bestseller and was published in forty-three languages. In the space of two years, I was on all the chat shows in the United States and had my own series on ITV.

Yet as all this was happening, my health began to fail. I was hospitalised several times, and my family thought I was going to die. A fourteen-book, three-movie deal worth millions couldn't keep sickness and depression from my door and from nearly destroying my faith.

The other great irony of my getting tossed out of school was this: One of the teachers from the school told a reporter that the children had become "excitable" after my talk. Imagine that – students being excited about reading. I wish that someone had made me excited about reading when I was ten or eleven. It might have saved me a world of trouble.

Then again, if they had, I wouldn't have this story to tell.

This is how I remember my life – through eyes that are prejudiced – it may not be how you recall it.

1

DROWNING

In the summer of 1957, my father went out one night and had more than a couple pints of Guinness at the Newlands Pub in Scarborough, where he worked as a barman. He came home in a jovial mood, and nine months later, on 3 May 1958, I was born.

At least that's the story as he told it, and I tend to believe him. My parents were both older when I was born; my dad, Frank, was fifty-three, and my mum, Mary, was forty. They'd already had three children before I came along – a boy who died in infancy and my two sisters. There's a long gap between my sisters and me, and I learned that my arrival came as a bit of a shock.

My parents were hardworking, loving people. My dad was about five feet eight, with olive skin, jet-black hair and blue eyes. His family came from York, and his grandfather had come to Scarborough to work as a postman. My dad's father was a policeman. My mum's family came from Ireland, and she was born in Paradise, a section of Scarborough that overlooks the town's south bay. Her dad was in the Coast Guard, and they lived in the row of Coast Guard cottages at the top of a hill, not far from Scarborough Castle and St Mary's Church, where Ann Brontë is buried.

My dad was one of the hardest-working men I have ever known. During the week, he'd get up at six o'clock, wash, dress and then be off to work at seven at a shoe factory, where he was a cobbler – or a mender of bad soles, as I like to think of him. He would work a full day, come back at six o'clock at night and have dinner, then he'd get washed and changed, and by seven he was at his second job, at the Newlands Pub. Though he was deaf, he'd learned to lip-read, and that's how he took his customers' orders. He'd get home around eleven, go to bed and start it all over again the next morning.

Because he worked so hard, the only time I ever really saw him was at three o'clock on Sunday afternoons. He had to work Sunday lunch at the pub, so he would get up early and take care of the bar cellar work. Then he'd tend bar in the pub from eleven till about two o'clock and be home by three. My mum would have his dinner on the table when he arrived. He would always bring home a walnut cream for me. It's a kind of candy – a curl of chocolate filled with cream, with a walnut on the top. I would always give him my walnut because he loved them.

My dad never said much at those dinners, or anytime really. He spoke very little and communicated mostly in sign language. On those Sundays, I would sit with him for a while, then take my walnut and put it in his hand. And that was literally my relationship with him for the first ten or eleven years of my life because he was always working. My mum was a canteen assistant and a cook in my local school, so I saw more of her, but not much.

As a child with a profoundly deaf father and a mother who was hard of hearing, very little verbal English was spoken in my home. My mum was constantly communicating with my dad in sign language, but she would speak to us kids in English.

Some children are angels. From their earliest days, they fill their parents' hearts with joy and laughter. They make up songs as they run through the house, and their giggles echo through the back garden when they are at play. For the most part, they follow their parents' instructions. When they disobey, they cry and say, "I'm sorry, Dad" or "I won't do it again, Mum, I promise."

But other children are spoiled brats. I'm sure I don't need to describe their behaviour, as no doubt you have come across them before. Yes, I was one of those, and from a very early age, I did what I wanted to do, not what my parents told me to do.

My earliest memory is of being three years old and having holes in my trousers. The holes were courtesy of our dog, a boxer whose name I can't recall and whose main job seemed to be keeping me in the back garden of our house on Maple Drive. We lived on a council estate, a row of about fifty terraced brick houses that were all joined together and ran along an abandoned railway line.

When my mum let me play outside, she gave me a strict warning not to leave the back garden. To make sure I followed her instructions, she let the family dog out to watch over me. Somehow the dog knew I wasn't supposed to leave, and if I went towards the gate, he would start growling. If I kept going, he would bite me on the bum and pull me back in. I'd try to pull away, and the dog would hang on – leaving holes in my trousers.

But I wasn't going to let a mere dog stop me. One bitterly cold winter afternoon, I was wrapped up tightly in my winter coat and hat, and I wanted to go out of the garden. As I got close to the gate, the dog bit me again. I turned around, and before he could react, I grabbed him by the leg and bit so hard that he ran off. I opened the garden gate and went on my merry way.

Since my sisters were much older than I was, they were assigned the job of looking after me when my parents were out. From what I can remember, they did that a lot. My sisters were good to me and were even prepared to fight the bigger kids when I got into trouble. And if I was sick, my mother would often keep my oldest sister home from school so she could watch me while my mum was at work. She and I were very alike, although she was six years older, and she often got the blame for stuff that I had done. She protected me, even if it meant she would get belted in my place.

Though we lived on the council estate, my parents made sure that my sisters and I never went without. We had plenty of food and new clothes. I had a pair of jeans, a set of playing-out clothes, a set of nice going-out clothes and a school uniform, and that was really all I needed. My parents also made sure my sisters and I never felt neglected and always had toys and gifts at our birthdays and Christmas. Looking back, I think that even my sisters went without so I could have what I wanted.

Our house was small but sturdy, made of red brick from the Ravenscar Brick Company. Going through the front door, you entered a small hallway, which was about six feet by six feet, and faced a set of stairs that ran straight up to the three bedrooms. Turning at the bottom of the stairs, you entered a sitting room, our main room, which was about twelve feet by ten feet. Next to it was the kitchen, about nine feet by seven feet, which you passed through to reach the toilet, which was about eight feet by five feet. And that was the whole house.

In my small bedroom, about eight feet by ten feet, the wallpaper changed every three or four years. As a young child, I had wallpaper with airplanes from the Second World War on it. At that time, my favourite thing was my tape recorder because I could record songs from the radio and listen to them in my room.

The sitting room was bare; it held a fireplace with a gas fire, a cabinet to one side, along with a sofa and my dad's big chair, which was placed right in front of the television. We never had lamps in our house. The main light, or what we called the "big light," was always on. Because my dad was deaf and, when he was older, partially blind, he used to sit very close to the television in our sitting room. My mum was hard of hearing too, so the TV was on at full volume all day. You could hear my house around the corner due to the constant noise from the TV, and we heard it even when we went to bed.

The television was our only source of entertainment. We didn't have many books, as neither of my parents was an avid reader. Before our television arrived, some of my friends and I used to stand outside the window of a neighbour's house and pray that she didn't close the curtains, because she had the only colour television on the street. We peered in and watched football on the screen, listening to the roar of the crowd coming over the speakers. It was fantastic. Then when our black-and-white rental set arrived, I was amazed. My friends and I wondered if there were little elves working in there, creating these pictures; it seemed like a magic box to us.

The day was 13 April 1965, and its events will forever be burned into my memory. I was a few weeks shy of my seventh birthday and had tagged along with my sisters as they and some friends set off for a day out along the Scalby Beck, which runs from the river Derwent to the North Sea. We were going to the weir – a concrete, artificial waterfall about two miles from our house – a good spot for picnicking and playing. It's a lovely wooded area where sycamore, holly, beech and other trees surround the beck. My sisters were forced to take me along since my mum wouldn't let them leave without me.

Once we got to the beck, my oldest sister told me very clearly to stay away from the water. She had just completed her lifesaving training, and she said in her firmest lifeguard voice, "Graham, don't go near the water." She was looking out for my own good, as I hadn't the slightest idea how to swim. But I just ignored her.

While my sisters and their friends were busy building a fire, I clambered up to the edge of the weir to catch some fish. I'd brought a jam jar with me, hoping to scoop up some minnows or tadpoles and bring them home. Some minnows were swimming just below the surface of the water, so I leaned over with my jar. Just a few more inches, and I'd have them.

The concrete wall was covered with moss and was very slippery. I leaned too far and slid into the water. It all happened so fast that no one saw me fall in. I sank straight to the bottom, about ten feet down because the weir is designed to hold water so that the river level is higher upstream.

Panic immediately came over me. I started thrashing my arms and legs in a frantic attempt to get back to the surface, but it was useless. The water was too deep, and besides, the force of the river was pressing me back down towards the weir. I sank back among the seaweed at the bottom of the beck.

I'm drowning, I thought to myself. *This is it.*

It was a bright, sunny day, and I could see the sunlight streaming into the water and the tree branches hanging just above. I stretched out my hands for those branches in vain hope, as if somehow I could reach them. But it was futile.

Several strange things began to happen. A sense of peace and warmth washed all over me. I knew I was drowning but didn't really worry about anything, because there was nothing I could do except literally go with the flow.

Then I felt like I was being dragged towards the surface as if I were a fish and something, or someone, was reeling me in. Suddenly I was above the surface of the water, looking down at the body of a young boy. His mop of ginger hair was floating around his head, and his hands were outstretched.

Where's he come from? I wondered. *There are two of us drowning here.* As the distance between the boy and me grew further, I realised that the boy was me and somehow I was out of my body. Everything seemed to get brighter the further I moved away from my body, though I didn't see a tunnel or any of the other sights that reportedly go along with near-death experiences. Below me, my body floated in the water as I drifted away into the sky.

Then suddenly I was back on the shore, puking up all the water I had swallowed. My elder sister had dived into the beck and pulled me from the water. I was alive. I suppose I should have been grateful to be alive, but the only thing I could think of was how awful I felt after spitting out all that water.

To my little six-year-old mind, the most traumatic part of the day wasn't nearly dying but afterwards when I had to walk the two miles home in some of my sister's friends' clothes. Someone lent me a pair of shorts, and someone a jumper. I remember walking up the road in this jumper, which was about ten times too big and was hanging down like a dress. Not the look I was after!

My sister ran ahead to tell my mum what had happened. When I got in the house, she was furious and told me off for getting my clothes soaked. She also told off my sister for not looking after me. She didn't realise that my sister had actually saved my life.

All that day and the next day, people kept coming round the house. They'd heard the story – that I'd drowned and my sister had saved me – and wanted to find out if it was true. Then my mum realised the depth of the experience. She wrapped her arms around my sister and thanked her for what she'd done.

A few days later, I got my first exposure to the media. Word had gotten around that a little kid from Maple Drive had drowned in the river and his sister had brought him back to life. Before long, someone from the local newspaper showed up at our door.

I was playing out in the back garden when my mum called me into the house. Inside was a strange man, wearing a trilby hat and carrying a notepad. A photographer was there as well, and as the reporter started asking questions, something about him terrified me, so I just turned heel and ran back to the garden. The next day, the headline in the paper read, "Girl, 13, Saves Drowning Brother."

I never told anyone about my out-of-body experience. It frightened me, and I didn't know what had really happened. Had I imagined it all? Or is something actually out there after we die? These questions would haunt me for years. This wasn't the kind of thing I would have thought to ask my mum about. She and my dad believed in God, but faith and spiritual matters weren't things we discussed at our house.

We didn't go to church, so I didn't have anyone there to talk to about it either. People on our council estate didn't attend church; it wasn't part of the culture. For one thing, the nearest church was a ways off, and not many people on the estate owned a car. The churches were in better parts of Scarborough, in middle-class neighbourhoods. We were working class, and for us, church just wasn't relevant to our daily lives. It was a place to go only when you were baptized, when you were married and when you died (for your funeral). Sunday morning was for doing other things. I didn't know what time church services were held, or even what people did when they were at church.

But my close encounter with drowning left me convinced of two things. First, death was real, and someday it would claim me. And second, I would have to find someone who could tell me if there really is something after death.

But it wasn't going to be the local vicar. In the Church of England, the vicar is supposed to care for the whole community, not just for the people who show up on Sunday morning. But he rarely came to our housing estate. In all the years I lived there, I think I saw him only once. I'd have to look elsewhere for the answers to my questions.

I lived out my early life in a fantasy world of cowboys and soldiers and strange creatures from other planets. My friends and I would play amazing games with bits of wood and cardboard boxes. My favourite was the Lone Ranger.

One Saturday morning, my friend Chris Metcalfe and I were at the Odeon Cinema with a couple of hundred other kids. There were no television shows for kids on Saturday mornings, so the Odeon, a big, thousand-seat cinema up by the railway station in Scarborough, showed movies for kids. We'd get there between half past nine and ten o'clock and watch the short movies and cartoons. Chomping on popcorn, we'd watch Superman, Dan Dare, Flash Gordon and Tom and Jerry on the big screen for a couple hours. Sometimes they'd show American westerns, like the Lone Ranger or Roy Rogers, which were my favourites. Then on the way home, we'd act out what we'd seen.

In the adventure shown on this day, the Lone Ranger approached the canyon entrance, his six-barrel gun drawn, his horse Silver just a few feet behind him. Trouble was nearby, and he knew it. High above, a group of Apaches looked down on him. One drew his bow back and launched an arrow that landed right between the Ranger's feet. Our hero jumped back, and the whole cinema seemed to gasp at the same time. What would he do?

When we got back to Chris's house, he found a bow-and-arrow set, which he gave to me. I clambered up on the coal house to be the Apache brave, and he stood in the garden, playing the Lone Ranger. I took aim, pulled back on the bow and fired the arrow at Chris. I hit the mark – it went straight through his shoe and into his foot. He started hopping up and down on one foot, trying to get the arrow out, howling and screaming like a banshee. At first I thought he was playing, but then I looked down and saw the blood spurting out of his foot. I panicked and started running, only stopping when I got home.

Chris's foot ended up being okay. The real trouble was that he'd been wearing a pair of brand-new shoes. It was the end of the summer holidays, and his new shoes were for going back to school, but now they had a huge hole in them and were stained with blood. My mother had to pay for the shoes, which put a big dint in the finances. Chris's family was just like us – they were close to the edge financially – and someone had to come up with the money. My mum found the money somehow, but she wasn't too pleased with me. Thankfully, Chris forgave me, and we remained great friends.

Looking back, I can see how my relationship with my parents worsened when I started going to school and making friends who didn't live on the council estate. Most of my school friends had parents who were younger and better off than mine.

It didn't help that most weeks, I saw more of my friends' parents than I did my own. I used to spend a lot of time at my friend Steve Kendall's house. He lived about a mile away, and his family owned their house. I idolized Steve's dad, Dennis, because I thought he was the father I wanted to have. He had a regular, nine-to-five job, and when he got home he spent all of his time with his kids. He'd take Steve on outings, and I'd go along sometimes, but all the while I'd be feeling bitter towards my Dad, wishing he wasn't working so that he could take me out.

The biggest difference was that Steve's dad didn't have any problem talking to him. My father could speak well, but his deafness was a barrier to full communication, and if I am honest, it was easier not to speak than to speak. I now regret this because I know that my dad was as good as any other, and I missed out on so much in our relationship.

Only many years later did I learn that my dad had to work two jobs because he had been married before; he was supporting two families. He didn't get paid a great deal as a cobbler, maybe ten or twelve pounds a week, and he had a lot of financial commitments that I didn't know about.

My dad never complained about how hard he had to work – he never really said much about anything. But he was gone most of the time, and that left a hole in my life. That hole grew deeper and wider with each passing year, until finally a great chasm stood between us. I now feel that this was of my making, and if I had thought of others instead of myself, things could have been different.

Because of my dad's never-ending work schedule, all the small graces and everyday routines that bind a father and son together were not available to us. I can't remember doing the father-son thing at all. Perhaps we did and I have blocked it all out in some way. But I can't remember my father ever tucking me into bed at night or telling me a story to ease my way into sleep. I never sat on his knee while he tied my shoe or held his hand as he walked me to school. We never went out into the back garden to kick a football, and my dad didn't run beside me during my first tentative attempts at riding a bike. We never even sat together on the sofa and watched television. For years, we were literally strangers to one another. He worked to get the family what we needed and me what I wanted, but I resented him for not being there.

Sometimes I would walk to the end of Maple Drive where it met up with North Leas Avenue and look across the road to the houses there. It seemed like another world; the homes were semi-detached – two houses together – cars were in the driveways, and mothers and fathers were home with their kids. I'd stand there and imagine what it was like to live in one of those houses.

One day the newspaper carried an advertisement for apartments for sale, not too far from where we lived. The advert said a three-bedroom apartment cost about four thousand pounds. I carried the newspaper to my mum, asking her why we couldn't live in a place like that.

"Graham," she said with a sigh, "you just don't understand. You don't know how life works."

What she meant was that we didn't have the money to buy something like that. Four thousand pounds seemed like just a little bit of money to me, but to my parents, it would have been a fortune.

My anger towards my dad started to come out in the way I treated my parents. When I was about nine or ten, my sisters got married and moved out of the house, and I was the only one at home. I really missed my older sister and would have done anything to stop her going. She was more than a sister; she was a friend and protector and someone I admired.

My parents had always spoiled me because I was the child of their old age, and things grew worse when my sisters were gone. I began to treat my parents badly, demanding that they buy me whatever I wanted. If I didn't get it, I would throw a tantrum and curse them, so they usually gave in and got me what I wanted, whether it was a new cricket set, an electronic train set or some new gadget for my Action Man figures.

My mum had bought me about six Action Man figures, which are like the GI Joe figures sold in the United States. I had a soldier, a sailor, a pilot, a mountain climber and several others, plus uniforms and other accessories. One day I got bored and decided to light them on fire. My dad kept spare fuel for his lighter in the kitchen, so I pinched the fluid and took it out to the back garden. I pulled the heads off my Action Man figures, poured lighter fluid in them, replaced the heads and then put them in a trench I'd dug. Once I had them all arranged, I soaked a piece of string with lighter fluid to serve as a fuse and lit it on fire. When the flame hit them, the volatile lighter fluid made the Action Men light up with a whoosh. Within a few minutes, I was left with a pile of burnt Action Man corpses. This was the kind of ungrateful thing I'd do with the things my parents bought me.

My dad lost his job at the shoe factory when he was sixty. He was given a small pension and was sent home. He was a very proud man and went out looking for a new job, but there wasn't much call for a sixty-year-old, out-of-work cobbler. Eventually he went to the council, was offered a job as a road sweeper and took it. My parents didn't tell me the details of his new job; they just said he was working for the council.

I found out what he was doing from some kids at school. Some guys came into the classroom full of kids and said in a loud voice, "Hey Taylor, we've just seen your dad. He's working for the council, isn't he?"

"That's right," I said.

"Do you know what he's doing?"

I thought he was working on the roads or in the water department. I said something to that effect, and they started laughing at me.

"No," they said, "your dad's a road sweeper."

I was humiliated. All of their dads were professionals – doctors, lawyers, teachers and things like that. So they laughed at me for having a road sweeper for a dad. I didn't come to my dad's defence but became more and more angry with him. I blamed him for making me a laughingstock. From then on, he and I grew even further apart.

My dad didn't last long as a road sweeper. He got sick, developed cataracts and eventually went blind in one eye. That ended his working career, so he became a househusband for my mother, while she went out to work.

Now that he was home, he tried to reach out to me. When I came home from school for lunch, he would make sandwiches for me and try to talk to me, but I had already shut him out. And if he tried to tell me what to do, we'd argue and I'd push him out of the way.

About the time that my dad's job was made redundant, some missionaries showed up on our housing estate. We first saw them on a Friday afternoon, right after school let out, in the fields behind our school. They were sitting out there playing their guitars, and some of us went over to see what was going on and to cause mischief, more than anything. They were all in their twenties and were singing and laughing with one another. They asked us if we wanted to join in the singing, but I thought the song had dodgy lyrics, and they kept repeating a swear word: "Jesus." In my language, Jesus was a curse, not something we sang about.

"What are you kids doing tonight?" one of the missionaries asked. They were having a meeting at a nearby church and wanted us to come.

"I'm not getting involved with some church," I told them and started to walk away.

"It's up to you," they said, "but there will be games and food."

Playing along, I asked, "What time does the meeting start?" If I was interested, I couldn't let any of my friends know.

"Seven o'clock," they said.

"All right, we'll be there."

As we walked away, I asked my mates if any of them were going to the meeting, and they all said no. Chris said that he was staying home, and I said, "Right, then I am staying home too."

But at about five minutes to seven, I showed up at the Methodist church in Scarborough, about a mile from my house, and there were all of my mates. We kind of all looked at each other as if to say "You liar – you came!"

The meeting started off with food: hot dogs, biscuits, lemonade and so on. Then they used the height of that time's multimedia technology – a slide show. Someone turned on some music and dimmed the lights, and they began to project slides on the wall. We saw a cartoon of a man carrying a sack, which he kept filling with all sorts of problems, hurts and pains. The more he filled up the sack, the more stooped over he became. Then he started dragging this sack up a hill, one step at a time. When he got to the top of the hill, he saw a cross. There he nailed the sack to the cross and then ran down the hill, freed of his heavy load.

After the lights were back on, one of the missionaries got up to give a talk.

"Look," he said, "this is the story of our lives. We all have things that hurt and are painful. If we give them to Jesus, he can set us free."

Someone put a banner up on the wall behind him, and it had a prayer written on it. "Dear Jesus," it read, "I admit that I'm a sinner and that I've done wrong. Please come into my life. I want to be born again. Fill me with your Holy Spirit. I want to follow you from this day on."

As the man read that prayer, I could feel panic rising. The slide show seemed to be about my life – I had built up so much resentment towards my mum and dad that it was overwhelming me. I also harboured a dread of dying, ever since the day I'd almost drowned, and woke up many nights worrying about it. All of that resentment and anxiety was dragging me down.

I started breathing heavier and heavier, thinking, "I've got to get out of here. I've got to get out of here." I jumped up and ran for the door, sprinting down North Leas Avenue. I stopped at a bus shelter about two hundred yards from the church, just by the Scout hut. Tears were streaming down my face. I got down on my knees and cried out to God, repeating the prayer I'd heard at the Methodist church.

"Jesus," I said, "if you're out there, come into my life. I want to be a Christian. I want to follow you. Come into my life right now."

When I got back home, I was still upset. I told my mum what had happened, about the slide show and praying the prayer in the bus shelter.

"Oh, that was so stupid," she said. She wasn't being nasty; she just didn't think it was necessary. She'd had me baptized when I was a baby, and I was a Christian in her eyes.

But I didn't believe her. "That's not enough," I said. "There has to be something more."

The next day, a youth minister turned up at the back door of our house. It was a windy day, my mum's washing was blowing around on the line just behind him, and there was this bloke saying, "Are you going to come back to church? What happened to you? We saw you were upset."

Mum grabbed me and pushed me inside, and then she told the man off. "Go away and leave us alone. Don't come around here anymore; just leave us alone." She was trying to protect me; she was afraid I was getting mixed up with some kind of cult or some odd group like Jehovah's Witnesses.

I snuck back to the Methodist church a few times, but it wasn't the place for me. The people were very nice and tried to welcome me in, but I knew I didn't belong. All of the kids in the church were from better neighbourhoods. I was the only one from the council estate, and being in church reminded me of everything I hated about my life.

My first experience with the church had a lasting consequence: it opened up a whole new spiritual dimension for me. Ever since my near drowning, I'd been terrified of dying. Sometimes I would wake up panicked in the middle of the night because of nightmares about dying, or I would lie awake, afraid to close my eyes for fear that I might not wake up. Even as a teenager, I was frightened of the dark and would sleep with the light on.

The worst part about nearly dying was the many questions that I couldn't seem to get answered. I came close enough to dying to know that something happened when we die but not close enough to have any answers. And I wondered if it had all been an illusion and if we just fade away into nonexistence when we die. That thought was more than I could bear.

I was terrified of death, and these Christians said there was life after death, but they didn't seem to know exactly what happens. I remember asking someone at church if we really went to heaven when we die, and he said, "I really don't know." That uncertainty, along with my embarrassment about being a kid from the council estate, kept me away from church.

So I decided I'd have to find some other answer to what happens when we die. From that time on, I got involved in anything having to do with the supernatural.

2

THE OTHER SIDE

I n my search for answers about what happens when we die,
I next went looking at the Spiritualist churches in Scarborough. There mediums claimed to communicate with spirits of
people who had died. Spiritualism was founded in the 1840s by
the Fox sisters of Hydesville, New York, and it enjoyed a revival
in Scarborough during the Second World War. Many people lost
loved ones during the war and were desperate for news of them.
People wanted to know whether their husbands and fathers
were alive or dead. If the War Department couldn't provide the
answer, people would go to the Spiritualist churches for help.
The Spiritualists would say either "Yes, I have seen him, he is
on the other side" or "No, he is not on the other side." Either
way, the Spiritualists would give people hope; they offered the
possibility of communicating with departed loved ones or the
reassurance that loved ones were still alive.

Since communication was often so difficult in those days, no
one could verify whether the Spiritualists were right or wrong.
But the hope they offered was attractive to people who were
desperate for news of their loved ones, so interest in Spiritualism grew greatly. It waned in the postwar years, but three
Spiritualist congregations were still in Scarborough when I was
growing up: one on Queen Street, one on Bar Street and a third
down in Westborough.

For me, the attraction of Spiritualism was that it seemed to offer easy answers to the questions about life after death and instant access to those on the "other side."

I was fourteen when I first stepped into a Spiritualist church, and the odd thing was, it looked much like the Methodist church I'd visited when I was younger. It was very plain, with wooden chairs and a table at the front with a cross and an offertory bowl on it. They sang songs about Jesus and prayed to him. Victorian paintings of Jesus hung on the wall. People believed that Jesus was a Spiritualist who contacted the Holy Ghost (for the Spiritualists, the Holy Spirit was literally a ghost that they could get in touch with).

That meeting, like most of the Spiritualist meetings I went to, was rather boring. There were no unexplained knocking sounds from spirits (something the Fox sisters were famous for), levitations or anything else out of the ordinary. Instead, the meeting consisted of a hymn, a Bible reading, a prayer and then a time of quiet, when everyone just sat listening. I sat in the front row, hoping to get a good view when something happened. Nothing. Finally a leader got up and introduced the medium who would serve as the speaker that evening.

The medium started into a routine, which was typical of all the meetings I went to. He began by saying something like, "I feel someone is here with the letter *K*. Does that mean anything to anyone?"

The medium would speak in a warm and inviting voice, panning the crowd for responses. If someone did speak up, the medium would start into a series of questions designed to draw information out of the person.

"Is the person in spirit or not in spirit?" (In spirit meant "dead.")

"In spirit, okay. Is it a man or a woman?"

"A woman? Is it Ka . . . ?"

The medium would keep it up until the person blurted out the name or some other identifying information.

I found the whole thing confusing. And I don't think the Spiritualists knew what to make of me. I was usually the youngest person there, and most of the time people ignored me. I would purposely sit in the front, hoping they would see me or have a message for me. But that never happened; it was as if I was invisible.

Once I started going to Spiritualist churches, I was so desperate to contact the dead that I got involved in having Ouija-board sessions with my friends and going into graveyards. Neither came to any good. I terrified myself further, and the nighttime became even more foreboding.

The trips to the graveyard were disappointing. A group of us would traipse there at night, waiting to see a ghost and hoping that a spirit would get in touch with us. We would hold hands, like in a séance scene in a horror movie, and someone would ask in a melodramatic voice, "Is anybody there?" Once in a while the breeze would blow through the trees and make an odd sound or someone would say, "I feel something," in an attempt to wind the group up. But nothing ever came of it.

The Ouija-board sessions, on the other hand, were terrifying. We'd tell ghost stories and then turn off the lights, light candles and get each other worked up. The power of suggestion – that this board was going to speak to us – is remarkable, and when you get a bunch of teenagers together in that kind of setting, you begin to feel that something creepy is happening. Sitting around a table, surrounded by shadows and flickering candles, we put our hands on the piece of glass, and before long, it seemed to move on its own, pointing out messages to us. I would become sure that we'd made contact with some supernatural creature, and panic would set in. Would this creature come after us?

Teenagers aren't the only ones who get misled by the power of suggestion. The whole phenomena of Spiritualism captivated some of the leading scientists of Victorian times, including Alexander Graham Bell and Guglielmo Marconi, the Italian scientist who discovered radio waves. Marconi was convinced that the radio waves he was picking up were coming from the spiritual world. Arthur Conan Doyle, the creator of Sherlock Holmes, was fascinated with Spiritualism as well. People who are desperate for some glimpse of the other side are vulnerable; they see and hear what they want to see and hear.

But it's not all a hoax, and once the spell is broken, many people realise that the spirits are not as kind and loving as they made themselves out to be. Many a spiritual problem starts out with a seemingly innocent visit to a medium.

About the same time that I was visiting the Spiritualists, I was going to Westwood County Modern School, a place for kids who failed their eleven-plus exams. Westwood was a sink school, one that took in all the kids from the outlying estates. It was a place of low expectations.

The school was housed in a dark, cold, menacing Victorian building. It wasn't wise to go to the decrepit toilets there, especially if you were a younger student. The older boys would hang out and wait for the smaller students to come in. When one appeared, the older boys would descend on him like a pack of wolves. They'd hoist him upside down, stick his head down the toilet and pull the flush chain.

A typical day's routine went something like this: we'd arrive at school for the nine o'clock assembly, at which a teacher played a hymn on the piano and hoped we'd sing along. Then the headmaster would come in and give us a lecture, and then we'd be sent off to lessons – history, English, maths, geography, woodwork, metalwork, physical education. There was no great expectation for us to do any work during the lessons and no sanctions if we didn't, as long as we turned up. If we stayed out of trouble, we could coast through.

But from the beginning, I was in trouble at Westwood, mostly for fighting. Early on, I got into a fight with several of the older boys and landed in hospital – they smashed my head against the radiator and knocked me out. I can't remember now what the fight was about or how it started; most likely, boredom was the cause. And my mouth always got me into trouble. I tried to be nice, but somehow I always had to have the last word, and fists would fly.

One of the games we played was called levitation, an early form of crowd diving, now found at rock concerts. A group of five or six of us would surround a friend and lift him in the air, passing him back and forth above our heads. We were doing this with Nigel Stevenson when someone had the idea that we should dangle him out the window by his ankles. I think that someone might have been me.

Nigel was a fantastic guy, so it was out of stupidity rather than spite that we hung him out the window. Needless to say, he was upset, but with five of us hanging on to him, he couldn't stop us. All he could do was keep screaming, "I can't fly! I can't fly! Don't let me go!"

Surely when you're holding a guy out of a third-floor window by his ankles, some part of your brain should realise how silly and dangerous you are being. But I just laughed at the way Nigel was screaming and flailing his arms. Eventually we hauled him back inside, but not before a teacher saw us.

Soon afterwards we were herded into the headmaster's office for a lecture and then the cane. Once the headmaster heard the story, he asked if we had anything to say for ourselves.

We didn't, so he shook his head and crossed the room towards the wardrobe, where he kept two canes. The first was stiff and thick, and when it hit, it left us bruised and sore. The second was more flexible, a thin cane that whipped through the air and stung, but at least the pain was over more quickly.

As a frequent visitor to the head's office, I tried to come up with strategies for beating the cane. If I was fast enough, I could pull my hand away just before the cane made contact. But this strategy usually didn't work; he would see my hand move, grab my wrist and cane me harder. The pain was excruciating. Sometimes I would come out of there with swollen fingers and tears rolling down my face.

Being hit on the backside was better than on the hands. One teacher used a cricket bat, and he'd chalk the number four on the bat before hitting us. We wore charcoal-black trousers for our uniforms, and the bat would imprint the number on our trousers. If we got hit with the bat, we had to go back to his room at 4:00 p.m. with the chalk mark still intact. If it was gone, the teacher reasoned that he had not hit us hard enough, so he'd employ the bat again. So of course, if anyone we knew got the chalk four, we'd grab him and quickly rub his backside so he'd get another beating.

This form of punishment was painful, but it was better than other sanctions, such as being expelled, because once we had our beating, it was over and done with. The memory of the cane made us think twice, at least for a little while, before doing something stupid. Also, the head didn't tell our parents when we got caned.

The one class I enjoyed during this time was music, for although I don't have any talent as a singer and can't play any instruments, I love music of every kind. But even in my favourite class, I couldn't stay out of trouble. Something about me set my music teacher off – perhaps that I was constantly trying to antagonize him.

One day my music teacher had finally had enough. "Right, that's it," he said, pointing to me. "Come here to the front of the class."

When I got to his desk, he told me to hold out my hands. I did, and *whack*, down came the cane. There was no worry that my now swollen and aching fingers might impede my ability to play music.

The irony is that when I became vicar of Cloughton in the early 1990s, my former music teacher was the organist. I must be the only Anglican clergyman ever to be caned by his organist.

One afternoon, when the memory of the cane had worn off, I was sitting in mathematics class when our teacher stepped out of the room. Of all the subjects, maths was the worst for me. I just couldn't do it, and didn't want to.

As soon as our maths teacher was out of sight, several friends and I hurried up to his desk to have a look inside. Everyone, including the teacher, had old-fashioned, Victorian-style school desks with heavy lids on them. Gazing at the bits of paper scattered inside, I thought I would play a practical joke on the teacher. Inside my pocket was a book of matches, and before my friends could stop me, I lit a match and held it to a piece of paper. At first the fire spread slowly, but then it caught on.

I dropped the paper into the desk, slammed the lid down and ran back to my seat before the teacher returned. No one said anything. I think my friends were partly shocked at what I'd done and partly waiting to see the look on the teacher's face.

When the teacher came back in, the smell of smoke was hanging in the air. Trying to find the source, he opened the lid of his desk, letting in a rush of oxygen. The paper inside had been smouldering and now ignited with a whoosh, the yellow flame leaping out of the desk and causing the teacher to dive for the floor, a look of sheer panic on his face. We thought it was hilarious, a chorus of laughter ringing out from the class. But the laughter immediately died down when the teacher stood up, his face beet red with anger.

He was a huge man with thick curly sideburns and long hair, and he seemed even larger as he towered over the class, glaring at each of us and trying to ferret out who was responsible.

"Who did this?" he asked in a thundering voice.

All hands, including those of my friends, pointed at me. The next thing I knew, my maths teacher grabbed hold of my shirt collar, catapulting me out of the seat and dragging me down the hallway to the head's office. The teacher was a very strong man and drove a motorcycle to school each day, so I should have known better than to mess with him.

The head inflicted the worst caning of my school career – one that left me sore for days. Setting my teacher's desk on fire also got me expelled from school for the first, but not the last, time.

Thirteen is an unlucky number, or so people say. For me, my thirteenth year was the worst year of my life. All I can remember is that it was a time when my body was telling me I was a man, yet my brain didn't want to let go of childhood. David Bowie was all the rage, and I wanted to be just like him. Sadly for me, I was quite a porker as a kid, and Bowie was so slender that he was almost feminine in appearance. So I decided to stop eating. My mum would cook, and I would pretend to eat; it was easy, really. Very soon the weight was going, and I was stuck with not eating. When I looked in the mirror, I thought I looked the same even though I was shedding pounds. I still thought I was fat.

Bowie was then in his "Ziggy Stardust" stage; he had spiky hair and wore makeup, earrings and nail varnish. I followed suit. I pierced my ear, started to wear nail varnish and even dyed my hair pillbox red. I went off to school with my new hairstyle and was sent home about thirty seconds after I walked in the door. The headmaster was stationed near the door as we entered the school and stopped me in my tracks as I made for the hallway for my first lessons.

"Taylor, what have you done to your hair?"

"Nothing," I said.

"Go home."

That was it. At first I thought he was joking, but he was dead serious. No student of his was going to school with scarlet hair if he could help it. I had to go home till he could decide what to do with me. In the end, he had to let me back in because the hair colour was permanent. The choices were either to make me shave my head – a worse choice in the eyes of the headmaster – or to wait for it all to grow out. So for the next few months, I was this red-haired, punk kid who wandered around the school looking like a Christmas tree. I did it to gain a reaction. I didn't want to be like everyone else, but I did want to be noticed and accepted. Life was a struggle and fraught with issues that I didn't know how to face, so wearing makeup and dressing outrageously meant I got the attention I desired.

It was about then that I got beaten up. School was all about a pecking order – who was top dog – and we sorted out the pack by fighting. One day at lunchtime, I came back from home and was pounced on by a guy before I even knew he was there. He smashed my head against the corner of a brick wall. I woke up in the ambulance without a clue where I was.

Two weeks later, I was walking home late one night and was set on by a gang of skinheads. They didn't like the colour of my hair and wanted the "faggot" to have a beating. They succeeded. As I crawled home, they managed to kick and punch me all the way. All I could do was scream, convinced they would kill me. One of them tried to smash a bottle on my head but missed. I remember getting near to my house and my sister coming to the door – she was heavily pregnant and back home to have the baby. She saved my life.

The guy ended up getting six months in jail, and I got a dislocated shoulder and two cracked ribs. He was out in four months and came to see me again. My ribs had just healed and I was playing cricket when I spotted him walking towards me. Something in me snapped. I picked up the bat and held it above my head, screaming at him that if he took another step, I would kill him. Tears streamed down my face, tears of terror and frustration at my own weakness. He left me alone.

Then a week later, it all happened again. Friday was fight club, and I got the call that another skinhead wanted to fight me, prompted by the guy who went to jail. They came to my class at the end of school and waited at the door. I couldn't run and would never dare go to a teacher for help. The skinheads wanted me to fight under the bridge next to the school. I quickly said that the only place I would fight was in the car park – which was near the police station; my plan was to run as soon as I got the chance. But the chance never came.

As soon as I got to the car park, the fight was on. The guy came for me and grabbed me by the hair, punching me in the face and then grabbing me by the throat. This was not going according to plan. He kicked me in the groin with his Doc's and then got me in a headlock whilst his mate robbed my pockets for what little money I had. Then he took out a picture of Bowie that I had folded up and tore it to pieces. It was his biggest mistake. For them, this was just another case of queer bashing, but for me, it became a matter of principle.

I'm not really sure what happened next. My perception is that a red veil fell on me, and my heart began to pound. I grabbed the guy by the ears and ran him to the wall and smashed his head against it. He fell to the ground, so I kicked him in the face and kept on and on until I was dragged from him. His last words were, "Enough ..."

His mates all scattered as a police car came down the street, but it turned without even stopping. I picked up the pieces of my picture and then saw to the kid I had just fought. I managed to get him back to his house and made sure he was okay. I just walked and cried, my body shaking as I wondered what was going to happen next. I was alone, and I didn't know who or what I was. I just felt I didn't fit in with anything. I realised then that I hated myself and who I was and yet couldn't do a thing to change it.

Amidst the self-hatred, my search for answers about life after death continued. After my disappointing visits to the Spiritualist churches, I turned my attention to the "myth and magic" shops that sold crystal balls, tarot cards and other books and materials on the occult. The Scarborough library had a section on witchcraft and magic, and that's where I first learned about tarot cards. After reading several books, I thought the cards might hold some answers to my nagging questions. I bought a set and practiced at home and then at school with my friends.

I would be practicing with my cards, and other kids would come up and ask me what I was doing. "I tell fortunes," I'd say, and inevitably they'd want me to tell them theirs.

Before too long, I'd have a queue of people waiting for me to tell their fortunes. So I'd look at the cards and say something like, "There's some disaster coming on in your life" or "Your true love will soon be here."

I didn't really know what the cards meant, so I'd just try to fill in the gaps and make things up. To be a good fortune-teller, I had to be a good listener; I had to figure out what the other kids wanted to hear and then tell them that the cards predicted just that.

Tarot cards and other occult practices ended up being a lot like drugs. With drugs, you start out dabbling with a bit of drink or a bit of blow, and soon you are into heavier stuff. In the occult, you start out with a Ouija board and tarot cards, and soon you can find yourself involved with some dangerous practices.

My hunger for answers seemed insatiable, so when I wasn't practicing fortune-telling, I was reading anything and everything I could about life after death and the supernatural. One Saturday, I was in the occult section of the Scarborough library when a man in his fifties struck up a conversation with me. Though I wasn't a Christian at the time, I'd taken to wearing a cross around my neck. The man pointed to the cross and asked if I was a Christian.

"Not really," I said.

"Why are you looking at all these books on witchcraft?" he asked.

"I'm really interested in all this stuff," I replied.

"If you're interested in witchcraft," he said, "you should come down to my shop. I've got some things you might want to see."

I was intrigued and promised I would visit later that week.

The shop was on my way home from school. When I stopped by, the man from the library was standing by the cash register. We talked for a few minutes, and he showed me some of his books on the occult. He began to teach me how to look up spells in them.

After a while he said something odd. "I think you're a medium," he said. "I think you can see dead people."

"Look," I replied, "I've been to the Spiritualist churches, I've heard all about this, and it's all a load of rubbish."

"Then look at my face," he said.

I stared at him and all of a sudden saw another image transposed over his face. This second face was of a dark-skinned man with a beard, dark eyes and black hair.

I jumped back, startled, wondering what was going on.

"That's my spirit guide," he said. "You can see him when you look at me."

I was unnerved but fascinated. I wondered if I had finally found something supernatural that I could take hold of.

Explaining exactly what happened in that shop is difficult. I believe I saw something but admit that I was so desperate to believe in something supernatural at the time that I can't be sure what it was.

I later learned that this man was the leader of a local coven of witches, or Wicca followers. I felt he played on my insecurities, for I desperately wanted some attention, to feel like I was unique and different. I was a skinny kid with low self-esteem and an easy target.

He said, "You've been brought here for a purpose because you have a gift."

That's how people involved in the occult work. They don't proselytize actively, but if someone shows an interest in the occult, they pounce, playing on the idea that the individual is gifted and was drawn to them by destiny.

The man said that if I wanted to find out more about witchcraft and talking to the spirits, he could show me since he was a witch who practiced Crowellian magic, named for a Victorian magician named Aleister Crowley. Crowley was a member of a magical organization founded by Samuel Liddel "MacGregor" Mathers, who was an associate of the poet William Butler Yeats. Crowley fell out with Mathers but became a proponent of "majick" and wrote influential books on tarot cards.

I began reading everything I could on the occult and writing out spells in a small black notebook. We finally had a collection of books in our house, but unfortunately it consisted only of writings on the occult, hidden in my room. I had other supplies as well – candles, incense and a "magical" knife.

I'd light candles, burn incense and then set fire to my spell, which was written on a scrap of paper. Most of the time it was something like, "I want Cindy or Susan to go out with me." The occult books described elaborate ceremonies, which I tried to follow.

I should make a couple of things clear here. Witchcraft is very dangerous, but witches – and I came to know many of them – can be very nice people. A witch is not a Satanist; Satanists are few and far between and hold to a completely different belief system. Witches, in contrast, are more pagan than they are satanic. They believe they are worshiping "Mother Earth" and the "horned God"; they believe that the devil is an invention of Christians and that they are not deliberately worshiping evil.

Witches may be kind, openhearted people, but I do believe that a negative force that Christians call Satan influences the whole area of the occult. When you practice witchcraft, you are inviting evil into your life. If you have tarot cards in your house, you might as well put a satellite dish on your roof and say, "Welcome, Satan," because it's an open door. As a priest, I have found that people who play with these things often reap the consequences; I certainly did.

Witchcraft also taps into a profound human need, one that few of us admit to having. All of us are going to die, and most of us are frightened about it. No matter who we are – Jew, Christian, Muslim, atheist – we want to know what will happen next. We want to know that someone or something is watching over us.

The way many liberal churches in the West practice Christianity means that they fail in answering these questions because any reference to the supernatural or the personal nature of God has been stripped away. In effect, they have neutered or castrated God. God has become an idea or a concept of "love," stripped of any ability to interact with the world, like a doting uncle who has wandered off. But a castrated God is of no use to anybody because he has no power to redeem and interact with us.

Through spell casting, the occult gave me a tangible way to interact with the spiritual world, and I expected results. I believed that something would actually happen as a result of my spells, that my pleadings were not falling on deaf ears. Someone was out there who would listen and respond. When I saw my circumstances change after casting a spell, that was proof to me that magic worked.

Many years would pass before I would realise that this is what New Testament Christianity is all about – a God who not only is powerful but also is willing to get involved in our lives. Not as some kind of automatic teller machine in the sky who would give me whatever I wanted but as a God who cares and who loves me so much that he would give everything he had to save me.

3

THE PENTHOUSE

In my life, often just the right person has come along at just
the right time to save me from myself. When I was six years
old, it was my sister who rescued me from a watery grave at the
bottom of the Scalby Beck. At fourteen, as I was self-destruct-
ing at Westwood, my history teacher came to my aid.

That man was unlike any teacher I had ever seen. Tall
and handsome, with a bronze complexion that reminded me
of the comic-book hero Doc Savage, he swept into the classroom on our first day of lessons and immediately captured our
attention.

"Turn off your televisions, boys," he said with enthusiasm in
his voice. Passing out our first reading assignment, he assured
us, "Just read this, and you will find a wealth of knowledge that
you can't get from a television."

When he lectured, he would bring history to life. We felt like
we were right there with Wellington, looking over the battle-
field at Waterloo; or battling the Luftwaffe in valiant Spitfires
high in the skies over London. A true orator, this teacher could
take a rough bunch of kids and enthral them with tales from
history. If any of us acted up, he would use his physical size and
strength to intimidate us. History Man (as I called him) was
everything I wished I could be.

His lessons were not limited to the classrooms either. An accomplished sailor, he took us on cruises from Scarborough Harbour into the North Sea; he also took us out on the moors to shoot rifles. I had never experienced anything like it. Here was a strong, bold man who also loved poetry and literature and had an exhaustive knowledge of world history. Suddenly a whole new world was opening up for me, with horizons far beyond the walls of Westwood and the confines of the council estate.

Unlike our other teachers, History Man had a wicked and sometimes risqué sense of humour. If we did well on a test or had an inspired debate, he would often reward us by telling a dark tale or a joke. Most of the time he had us eating out of the palm of his hand and made education enjoyable for an hour a day. Then the lesson bell would ring, and we would again be plunged into the conformity of another lesson with someone who didn't care for the young delinquents before them and who, like us, yearned for the home-time bell.

I had been drinking and smoking off and on since the age of twelve. A friend of mine used to pinch cigarettes from a shop and sell them to us for a penny each. In the early days, I wouldn't inhale, but before long, some of my older friends taught me that as well. That first deep breath of cigarette smoke seared my throat and lungs and made my head spin. On the way home, I was so dizzy that I could hardly walk and barely made it up the front stairs and into the loo before becoming violently ill. I was so sick I thought I was going to die. But the memory quickly faded, and the next day I was back smoking with my friends.

Like so many young lads who grew up around Maple Drive, my first drink came at the Scout dance, which was held every Saturday night at a local dance hall. One of my friends would bring along some cider, beer or sherry, and we'd drink it before going into the dance. The dance hall was right next to the bus shelter, where I'd once prayed to Jesus. But I set the memory of that night aside, as I found the drink and drugs more appealing. Getting drunk helped me forget my inhibitions and insecurities.

The more I got into drinking with my friends, the more my parents lost their influence over me. I was hanging out with a gang, leaving at six in the evening and not coming back till midnight. I may have been led astray, but I was more than willing to follow.

My mum would ask me what time I'd be coming home, and I'd say, "I'll be back about two or three in the morning." If they objected, I gave them two fingers and walked out the door, saying, "I do what I like, Mother, and I don't care what anyone says."

I believed that was true; I didn't think I had to listen to anyone. Not my parents. Not my teachers. Not the headmaster. The headmaster might give me canings, but he couldn't make me mend my way. But the History Man could.

History Man was a great teacher but had strict rules. If we broke them, we had to pay. When I came back from lunch one day after I had run a scam in his class, he was waiting for me. Some of the other students had grassed me up and informed on me.

"I need to talk to you," he said.

"What is it?" I asked, playing dumb.

He grabbed me and looked me straight in the eye. "Oh, you don't know what you've done?" It wasn't a question; he was challenging me to lie to his face.

"I know what I've done," I said.

He took me out back behind the school and gave me a good lathering. I was a big kid and wasn't afraid of anyone. Since I didn't listen to my mum and dad, I thought that no one could tell me what to do. But History Man showed me I was wrong.

After History Man's lesson, I changed my ways. If it hadn't been for him, I'd have eventually ended up in prison. At that time, when my life was out of control, he saved me from myself.

Even after I'd left school, History Man kept a watch on me. He knew that I was going wrong, that I was getting into sex, drugs and all the rest of it. "Graham," he told me, "you're not choosing a good life." Even then, his words would bring shame to my face. But I couldn't stop myself.

By some miracle, I earned four "O" levels at the end of my studies at Westwood, which opened the door for me to attend Scarborough Sixth Form College. Very few kids from Westwood made it out, and indeed it was touch and go whether the college would accept me. The school authorities were right to be wary of me. While my behaviour was now in check, my academic skills were woefully inadequate. I had no work ethic to speak of. I didn't do any homework and had never learnt how to revise or improve my schoolwork. My natural intelligence had compensated for my poor study habits at Westwood, where expectations were low. So the demanding academic environment at sixth form college was completely alien. And I had no interest in even trying to catch up to my classmates.

I did, however, discover two new things at sixth form college. I discovered books, which we never had many of in my house when I was growing up. And I discovered girls. By this point, my ideas about sex were in a mess. There was a girl on my estate who, for sixpence, would show you her privates. So at the age of ten, I was saving up my sixpences and going to visit her, thinking that this was wonderful.

Then a friend of mine sold me a pornographic book when I was about twelve, and he and some other friends of mine and I would spend hours looking at it. I now realise that this pastime was shared by many children of that age. But my problem was that my sex education came only from other kids, and some of the stories they told made me wonder how the human race had managed to survive for so long. Sex appeared to be a weird ritual that took place only after dark. I'm glad we didn't have any contact with real girls at that time; they were still alien creatures to us.

Then I met Caroline, a tall, blonde girl who seemed to spend all of her time at the library and was always carrying a big pile of books. I desperately wanted to get her attention. So I used to follow her around like a teenage stalker, and whenever I could make out what book she was reading, I would run to the library and check it out. I would skim the back cover to find out what it was about – because I didn't want to actually read the thing – and then position myself somewhere where Caroline would see me, book in hand. The first book I tried this with was George Orwell's *Animal Farm*.

When she came by, I looked over the top of my book, trying nonchalantly to get her attention. When she saw the book, she came over.

"Oh, hi Caroline," I said.

"Is that a book you're reading?" she asked with a hint of suspicion in her voice. Apparently my reputation for never reading had gotten around.

"Oh yeah," I said. "It's fantastic. Have you read it?"

That led to a long conversation about *Animal Farm*, which mostly entailed my listening to what Caroline thought about the book and me nodding my head in agreement. I realised that if I wanted to get to know all the hot girls at my school, hanging out in the library was the best way to do it. And before long, I was actually reading the books as well. I finished *Animal Farm* and moved on to *1984* and *Lord of the Flies* and then to the poetry of Ted Hughes and Sylvia Plath.

Lord of the Flies became my favourite. It is about a group of boys stranded on an island without any grown-ups. I wanted that to happen – to get rid of all the teachers, parents and adults and live on an island with all my mates, doing crazy things. My conversations with Caroline about books were a bright spot in my time at school.

I had other things to occupy my nights instead of homework, as I had landed a job in a Scarborough nightclub called the Penthouse. It opened in the 1960s, in what was once a second-floor billiard hall, on St Nichol Street in Scarborough. The building had previously housed the Lloyds Bank and before that was part of the town hall. Now a different class of people arrived, as punks and hippies had replaced bank managers and business-men as the main clientele. The club managers booked many of the up-and-coming bands of the day: Led Zeppelin, Manfred Mann, Yes, and even the Sex Pistols made the long journey to Scarborough to play there.

The Penthouse was a long room with a bar that stretched along one side of the room and a wooden dance floor on the other side. The rest of the floor was carpeted and was always soaked with beer, so our feet were constantly sticking to it. The place was filled with the smell of cigarettes and beer.

Because I was six feet tall when I turned fifteen, I convinced the bar manager to hire me as a glass collector. My job was to go around from table to table, pick up empty glasses and bring them back to the bar. Fairly soon I progressed to working as a waiter at the bar. I worked Wednesday, Friday and Saturday nights, and by the time I was done working and drinking, it would be two or three in the morning before I'd get home.

On Fridays, I'd arrive early and hang out in front of the club entrance, waiting for the band to arrive. We earned an extra three quid when we roadied the band in. Once the band arrived, I'd hump the gear upstairs, carry the guitars and amps and meet the guys as well. That's how I met people like Elvis Costello, the Stranglers and the Sex Pistols for the first time. Roadies also got free beer from the band, an added incentive.

When on 13 August 1976 the Sex Pistols arrived in Scarborough, I thought they were just another bunch of punks. After the show, I got invited to join them at the Central Hotel for drinks. Onstage, Johnny Lydon – or "Johnny Rotten" as he was better known – Sid Vicious and the rest of the band had angry, antisocial personas, but at the hotel, they were polite and gregarious hosts.

We had a great deal to drink that night, and I doubt that Johnny Lydon would remember me, as we were all worse for wear. But Lydon's intelligence shone through even then. I always thought he was the kind of guy who would do well as a member of the government because he really knew what made people tick. He was entertaining as well, because the drunker he got, the more excited he became. It was as if someone had flipped a switch, and he'd launch into a long monologue on politics or economics.

Spending my nights at the Penthouse meant I spent even less time and attention on schoolwork than before. While my academic performance was not winning accolades, my frequent absences were getting the attention of my teachers. My English teacher said in a report, "He contributes well when he is present, but he's been away too often to be much use."

My involvement with the occult got the attention of some of the Christian students at school. I was still doing my tarot-card readings at lunchtime and carried books on the occult with me. So several of the students from the Christian Union made me their project. I was the chief of sinners in their eyes, the representative of Satan, and I felt they would do all they could to have the demons cast from me and to see my soul saved. The lengths they went to were extraordinary, and looking back, I am thankful for their prayers and diligence.

Ruth was one of the leaders of the Christian Union and seemed completely fearless – a rottweiler for Jesus. Secretly I admired her. She had something I wanted, but I held back. I could never be a Christian; that would not be cool. So for the sake of fashion, I was prepared to follow a path that would lead to destruction. The sad thing was I knew it, but I was so trapped by the snares of the occult that I couldn't escape.

One day Ruth bounded up to me in the school dining room and pulled the tarot cards out of my hands, dumping them on the table. Then came the lecture: "You need to repent of what you're doing. You're going to burn in hell if you continue with this occult stuff."

She looked as though she meant business, and even I wasn't going to argue with her. Ruth was the darling of the football players, and one cross word from me would have meant summary execution in the shower room by her admirers. I also had a secret fear that she might be right and that her God was far more powerful than the creatures I was getting involved with.

I stood up and glared at Ruth. At six feet, I towered over her, but Ruth wasn't intimidated. She stared me down, as if daring me to go ahead and try something. When I realised that this crazy Christian girl wasn't going to back down, I turned away from her, picked up my cards and the rest of my school things and started walking away.

Once again, Ruth was in my face. "I'm going to pray for you, Graham," she said. "I'm going to pray that Jesus sorts you out. I'm going to pray that Jesus gets hold of your life and changes you completely."

"Don't start the Jesus bit with me," I told her. Not that I had anything particular against Jesus. From what I'd read of him, he was a good and holy man. Maybe not the Son of God, but a good man. These Christians, however, were another story. I wasn't about to get mixed up with them, for I thought Christianity was boring, irrelevant and untrue. When Ruth finally decided to leave me alone, I watched her go, muttering curses under my breath.

From then on, every time she saw me, Ruth would remind me that she was praying for me. "Oh, hi Graham," she'd say. "You still need Jesus." She said it in such a sweet voice that it was doubly irritating.

"Don't you pray for me," I'd respond angrily, aggrieved that someone should dare to think my life so bad that I needed God.

Ruth never batted an eye, no matter what I said. But she did pray for me for years. Looking back, it seems like God answered those prayers, though not for a very long time.

A few months later, I found a chance to get back at Ruth by asking her best friend to go out with me. To my surprise, she said yes. Even more surprising, when the date was over, she let me walk her home and invited me in. I was thrilled when I heard that her parents were away from home that night; my plans were coming together. After talking with her for a few minutes in the living room, I asked if she'd mind showing me around the house.

I made my move when we got to her bedroom.

"Do you know what is going to happen now?" I asked, reaching towards her. It was my naive intention to get back at these Christians by sleeping with one of them.

She pulled away. "Nothing's going to happen now," she said.

"What do you mean? We're here; there's nobody in the house. Who's going to stop us?"

Then she laughed at me. "Do you think I'm going to sleep with you? You must be joking. I like you a lot, but ..."

There was always a *but*; it meant "No way, never." The explanations came thick and fast. She said that she would have to be married to go *there*. I could see from the look on her face that she had no intention of that – well, at least not with me.

"What's marriage got to do with it?" I said, getting off the bed.

"You have to be married to have sex."

"Why?" I said. "I've slept with other people – marriage doesn't matter." I started feeling I was losing my chance, and my ego started to shrink.

I tried again, more desperately. "Let's just enjoy ourselves. We're young, we're free. Let's just do it." I frantically searched my limited knowledge of the Bible in the hope of finding a word for the situation. Love your neighbour as yourself came to mind but somehow didn't seem convincing.

"No, no, no," she said, taking my hands gently but firmly and moving them from her. "I'm not sleeping with you. Let me tell you about the Lord."

The *Lord* – there he was again, that stalker who pursued me like a hound, even into the bedroom of a hot date. Finally it dawned on me. This girl had lured *me* back to her house to convert me. Ruth and all her Christian friends were plotting to get me converted.

Everywhere I went, a gaggle of Christians would say, "You need Jesus. You need Jesus. You need Jesus." I felt like Jesus was doing a lot of advertising. And when I was trying to do wrong, here comes another Christian.

Jesus seemed to be pursuing me. I would see his name everywhere I went, and even when I tried to do the tarot, I would think of the cross. A nagging voice in my head started to tell me that what I was doing wasn't right. I became torn; I was pulled towards God on the one hand and dragged back into occult practices on the other by my desire to find the answers to the mysteries of life.

Around this time, I nearly killed myself. It was unintentional, but death was lurking at the bottom of a glass. Nick was a mate who later went on to play in a successful rock band, and it was his eighteenth birthday. Soon most of the drink was gone, and all that was left was an old and sweet bottle of sherry. There was nothing else to drink, but the night was young, so down it went.

Alcohol poisoning is a strange thing to experience. After the party, I woke up in a churchyard and thought I was dead. I shivered and shook and felt as if a small family of mice had taken up residence in my mouth. My eyes opened slowly to the bright morning sun and the sight of a little old lady with a small white dog, a Scottish terrier, peering down at me. My first thought was that if I was dead, then this must be God, or at least one of his messengers.

"Are you an angel?" I asked, wondering why there was no halo or heavenly choir. She greeted me with stone-faced silence.

After a few minutes, I realised that I was lying on her husband's grave. Then the events of the previous evening slowly trickled back into my mind. I had left my mate's house sometime after sunrise and started walking home. The climb up by the cemetery had left me winded, and spears of pain had stabbed my brain with every step. So the cemetery seemed a quiet place to get a little rest. Once I sat down, my back against the cool stone of a grave marker, the alcohol took over. I passed out in the early morning sunshine.

I beat a hasty retreat from the little old lady and walked the remaining distance home. Once there, I was violently ill for several hours. I clung to the toilet, my head a few inches from the water. This was sicker than I had ever been. For two days, I lay in bed, unable to stop shaking or to take more than a step or two without wanting to throw up. Lying in my bed, I swore that I would never drink again.

That pledge lasted all of three days. The party had been on Tuesday; I was out of bed by Friday morning and drinking again on Saturday night. Ah, the short memory of the addicted personality.

When I was seventeen, I had my first steady girlfriend. One thing led to another, and I began to spend more and more time at her place and less and less at home. I made enough money from the Penthouse to pay for food and booze, and crashing at her house meant I could avoid the hassles of trying to explain to my parents why I was home so late. I was so engrossed with my nightlife that I rarely woke up in time for school and would miss weeks of lessons at a time.

Near the end of my first year at college, I woke up one morning in time to make it to school. During my first lesson of the day, I was summoned to the headmaster's office. Sitting behind an enormous wooden desk, he motioned for me to sit in a smaller chair in front of him. As I sat down, I noticed an envelope addressed to my house on Maple Drive.

Before handing me the letter, he lectured me on how I had wasted my time and theirs. I had taken up a valuable space that could have gone to another, more deserving student. Then as he read from my year report, I realised I was in deep trouble. The pit in my stomach began to grow as he read from one of the tutors, "The fact that Graham did not even turn up for the exam is a suitable comment on his performance this year."

I frantically began to search my imagination for a suitable reply. Now that I was facing expulsion, I realised that this was not the conclusion I wanted. The writing had been on the wall, but in my search for a good time, I hadn't paid attention.

"You are finished," he said, in announcing my expulsion. "You have gone beyond your abilities."

Then, as though it were a consolation, he told me that only the top 15 percent of young people managed to get into university. I was obviously not of that calibre, and it was better not to waste time pretending otherwise.

"I want to talk to the school governors," I said, trying to think of something to put off what seemed to be my execution. "They'll give me a second chance."

He smiled with a hint of satisfaction on his face. "I've talked to the governors already. They agree with me. You're out."

If he had given me a second chance, I might have actually turned things around. But he wasn't a man prepared to give second chances.

Years later I was the celebrity guest invited back to the school to open a new learning centre, and ironically my name now adorns the wall on a brass plaque. God has a strange sense of humour and has replaced the years the locusts had eaten. Throwing me out was actually the best thing that happened because it was a needed wake-up call. But I'm sad to say that I soon slipped back into my old ways, and life became even darker and more complex.

4

ROCK AND ROLL

It was London, 1979, and I was twenty-one. The beer was nowhere near ready to drink; it had been fermenting for only about two weeks, but that made no difference to me or my mates. We had been drinking for several hours at a house in Battersea, London, and the alcohol coursing through our veins had dulled our senses enough to make the frothy mixture in the vat look appealing. Besides, I wanted a drink right then, and we'd already consumed every other bottle in the house. The only thing left was the batch of half-finished, home-brewed beer that was bubbling away in a back room.

Setting aside the top of the vat, I took a dirty mug and scooped out a pint of the brown, fermenting liquid. My friends joined suit, and over the next hour, we sat around downing pints of the smelly, clumpy brew. The beer tasted great going down, and we convinced ourselves, in the way that drunken lads often do, that it was fine to drink.

During the dark hours of the night, when the party was long over and I had staggered home, the half-fermented beer lay stewing in my belly. Eventually it made its way back out the way it had come in. For the next three days, it felt like the whole world was furry with yeast, and the slightest noise made me feel like someone was hitting me with a sledgehammer. It was by far my most horrible hangover ever.

My hangover was augmented by the aftereffects of the improvised pizza I'd prepared the evening before. The desire to eat often accompanied my partying. As food didn't play an important part of my life, the cupboards were often bare, and that night all I could find was a large box of pizza-dough mix, some mouldy cheese, old bacon and an onion that had already sprouted. Within the hour, I cooked all this into a large sloppy pizza, using ketchup as a sauce and adding a generous sprinkling of salt and pepper to make the whole thing edible.

Looking in the mirror the next morning, I couldn't understand why I was covered in white dust or why my face was smeared with red, sticky liquid. For the next several days, I spent most of my time sitting on the loo in the grimy washroom whilst the pizza that had given me food poisoning exited my body with the ferocity of a missile. I also discovered the joy of putting the toilet roll in the refrigerator to bring added comfort to sensitive areas of my body.

The effects of that dreadful hangover have been long-term. Even now I can't stand to be in a room where bread is rising or baking; the smell of yeast brings back vivid memories of that gut-wrenching experience.

Two years earlier, on a Saturday morning just after my nineteenth birthday, some friends and I had hired a van, packed in our few belongings and drove to London. Although we had rented a flat (sight unseen) over the phone, we had no grand plans or any concrete job prospects. Still, we left convinced that our fortunes lay in London.

I'd seen very little of my parents since leaving sixth form college. I'd gone home only occasionally once in a while when my clothes needed washing. At the time, most of the girls I was mixing with came from very wealthy families. Their houses had four or five bedrooms and were stuffed full of couches and paintings and all the trappings that come with wealth. In contrast, my parents' home on the council estate, with its bare walls and rented television, was a reminder that I didn't measure up.

My main obsession in those days was fame. I had no talent or ability. I couldn't act, sing or dance, write, tell jokes or do anything of the sort. But I told people that I was going to London, where I would be discovered and become famous. Of course, these were the puffed-up assertions of someone who felt completely inadequate. I was paranoid that someone would find out who I really was – even though I myself didn't know who I was.

Through my contacts with bands at the Penthouse, I learned that record companies were always looking for people to work in their promotions departments. Soon after arriving in London, I put on my best shirt and my best pair of blue jeans and knocked on the door of CBS Records, near Soho Square. When the receptionist answered, I told her I was looking for a job in promotions. One of the managers agreed to interview me, and I did well enough for them to let me work in telephone sales.

Each week we received five singles and two albums along with a list of music stores and radio stations to contact. The idea was to get DJs and record-store clerks and managers excited about the new records. The job was made easier because the bands we were plugging were great – Earth, Wind and Fire, Adam Ant, Bob Dylan.

To do the job well, we had to develop a rapport with the DJs and the store clerks and managers. I had a stash of gifts – watches, bottles of champagne, T-shirts and backstage passes from the bands – that I used to make people feel special. These "goodies," as we called them, were a way of greasing the wheels, of building relationships with customers. Human nature being what it is, it became a bit of a competition amongst people as to who could get the best deal.

We were paid a flat wage as well as a commission based on how many records we sold. We had competitions to see who could sell the most and got prizes and a monetary bonus if we won. Once the weekend rolled, we began partying right after work on Friday and kept going through Sunday.

For me, the best part of the job was my CBS identification card, which meant I could get into most shows at rock venues or nightclubs without paying. We'd go and watch a band, then afterwards make our way to a pub and spend the rest of the night falling down drunk. If my CBS card didn't get me in for free, I went back to being a roadie. Most of the bands I'd met at the Penthouse were playing in London, and often they remembered me. Being a roadie meant a free pass into the show and free beer.

The great thing about the punk era was that there was no separation between the audience and the band. And there was none of this celebrity crap that we have now, where bands are immediately whisked away after the show. In the 1970s in places like the Marquise or the Music Machine or the World's End, we were standing shoulder-to-shoulder with band members all of the time. If they weren't playing, they were watching the other bands. So standing there wearing leather jackets and tight jeans covered in safety pins, we'd have right next to us someone from the Sex Pistols, the Stranglers or the Clash.

We'd go from gig to gig, drinking, smoking and being on the lookout for the next hot band. I saw Sting in a pub in Islington at one point; I was standing just a few feet from him as he and his mates were thrashing away on stage. We could hardly imagine that he'd become an international superstar. Back there in Islington, he was still Gordon Sumner, the singing Geordie milkman with a dodgy haircut.

I moved around in London, hopping from flat to flat. I first shared a flat with my friends from Scarborough, the five of us crammed into a flat designed for one or two people. Since space was at a premium, my bed was in what we called the "conservatory" – a small niche in the hallway between the kitchen and the toilet. From there, we moved on to bigger and better flats, with a larger and ever-changing gang of inhabitants.

Things were fine as long as a party was going on. People were friendly on the surface, but everybody was out for their own ends, and friendships were thin. We were great drinking partners but not much more. Living a hedonistic lifestyle was all about the next drink or the next lay, not about deep and compassionate friendship.

Flat sharing always had a downside, especially when it came to the things that flatmates could do. For instance, back when streaking was in fashion, my flatmates encouraged me to strip and run. I was eager to please in those days, so I did it quite merrily; I also wanted to collect the winnings from the bet we'd made. The street where I lived was empty, so I slipped from my clothes into the cold, fresh morning air. I ran the length of the street and back again and was seen only by the gathering at the window of the flat. Little did I know that as soon as I took three paces from the door, they had locked me out.

When I reached the door, substantially chilled, I found it locked and bolted. I banged for many minutes as the laughter from inside increased and my confidence decreased. As I stood outside watching the pigeons fly from roof to roof, I started to laugh. Being naked in public is a very strange thing. It seems as if all of our personality is contained in the clothes we wear to make us who we are.

Another revelation of the level of friendship with my flatmates came when I developed a serious bronchial infection, a side effect of all the smoke and drink and my generally unhealthy lifestyle. The coughs wracked my body so intensely that I couldn't rest. My doctor gave me some cough medicine with codeine and ordered me to bed for a few days. It worked, and I finally fell asleep. When it wore off and the coughs returned, I dragged myself out of bed to get some more, but the medicine was missing. After some frantic searching, I found the bottle, now empty, in a bin. One of my concerned flatmates had drunk it to get a buzz from the codeine.

Eventually I landed at the head office at CBS, working near Soho Square in a building right next to a Hare Krishna temple. Nearby was a wine bar, and those who worked at CBS Records could go there and order a carafe of wine to get drunk at lunch.

One Friday in particular stands out in my mind. A launch party was held in the afternoon for the new record of a band that had some kind of French connection. I hadn't planned on staying for the party – the band was rubbish – and I was going to join some friends who were driving to Scarborough for the weekend. One of the friends worked nearby, and we were going to catch the tube together to meet up with the rest of the group. But at the last minute, I changed my mind. The office was filling with pop stars, free food and free booze, highlighted by girls in skimpy black outfits passing out bottles of French beer, and I didn't want to miss any of it. My motto at the time came from a Queen song: "I want it all; I want it now."

I called my friend and told her I'd be a little delayed. I said I was going to stay at the launch party for an hour or so and then meet up with her.

Several hours and many pints of French beer later, I finally set off from the office. One of the girls took pity on me – the French beer was really potent, and I was staggering down the hallway – and offered me a lift to the tube. I told her I needed to get to the Kilburn tube station, but either my speech was slurred or her hearing was off, because she dropped me at the wrong station. Before I realised it, she had driven off. I hadn't a clue how to get home. To make things worse, it was a hot summer's day, and the combination of the heat and the beer was too much for me. I collapsed by a wall near the station.

I woke up two hours after I'd left the launch party with no clue where I was. This was a common experience for me in those days, as I tried just about everything except heroin. Some of my friends had gotten hooked on heroin, and watching them turn from healthy twenty-year-olds into gaunt, worn shadows of themselves who lived only for the next fix was enough to frighten me away. Still, many mornings I woke up with no idea where I was or who the person next to me in bed was.

Getting up from the sidewalk, I started staggering down the road, hoping I was headed in the right direction but not exactly sure where I was going. About ten minutes later, a car pulled up, and the driver rolled down his window and told me to get in.

The alcohol-induced haze prevents me from remembering what he looked like or what kind of car it was. To be honest, I barely remembered my name at that point. I must have been coherent enough to tell him where I lived, because eventually the car pulled up in front of my flat. The driver opened the door for me, helped me out and led me to the doorstep. He rang the doorbell and then, just as quickly as he'd appeared, got back in his car and vanished.

I was completely vulnerable that afternoon. Anything could have happened to me – I could have been mugged or killed or arrested and locked up. But this stranger picked me up and took me straight home. I have always remembered his act of mercy and the risk he took in picking up a drunken, lost kid. Thank God for the kindness of strangers.

London life began to take its toll, and I was sacked from CBS for being a complete loser. The director said I was "too wild a child" after I had gone to a gig in a CBS limo and left them with the bill. I still wanted to work in the music industry and managed to get a job at Virgin Records. Employing me was one of Richard Branson's only mistakes.

Long before he was the "rebel billionaire" or setting world records flying hot-air balloons, Richard Branson was the guy who signed the Sex Pistols. Branson started Virgin Records as a mail-order business, later opening a shop and then a recording studio with the same name. He got his first big break when *Tubular Bells*, made at the studio by Mike Oldfield, became a smash hit. But what really brought Branson into the public eye was snatching up the Sex Pistols when their first record company dropped them.

In 1977, the Sex Pistols' version of "God Save the Queen" was banned by the government, which only made their song all the more popular. After their manager was arrested in a publicity stunt on the day of the Queen's silver jubilee in 1977 – the band launched into the song while on a boat on the Thames near the House of Commons – the Sex Pistols had the number one song in the country. At that moment, we felt that punk was going to become something more than a musical movement, that a young persons' revolution in Britain would take off, fuelled by punk rock. But the government clamped down because the music was so anarchistic.

I wanted to be where all the action was, so when a job opened up at Virgin, I leapt at it. Everything was bigger and better at Virgin – the pop stars, the paychecks and especially the parties. Richard really knew how to throw a party.

One night, in honour of his birthday, Richard threw a bash on his boat, which at that time was a river barge. We boarded at Little Venice and cast off, heading for the Camden lock. The boat was packed with about fifty people, mainly musicians and company employees, with plenty of free booze and food to go around. It was a beautiful evening, and I couldn't stop looking at Richard, amazed to be so close to such a major player.

Virgin was still small enough at that time for Richard to know everyone by name. We were all drinking and laughing when he turned to me at one point, saying eight fateful words: "Graham, do you want to drive the boat?" I had taken on board as many gallons of champagne as the boat had diesel and had never been at the helm of a boat before, so entrusting me with the safety of the barge was not an inspired decision. But the word *no* was not part of my vocabulary. So even though I was completely intoxicated, I happily took hold of the boat's wheel. All was well as long as the boat stayed in the middle of the canal and chugged along. The thing was, I didn't see the lock coming and steered the barge straight into the lock wall. One minute the party was in full swing. The next, champagne, food and celebrities were strewn across the deck. My Virgin colleagues – including Richard Branson – and their guests, were sent sprawling.

Thankfully, the boat, the lock and the passengers all escaped serious harm, as we were going very slowly. But my career at Virgin had suffered a serious blow. I don't think Richard liked the idea of me sending him and his guests scuttling along across the decks.

I didn't work for Virgin much longer. That was the beginning of the end of my life in London, as things were falling apart rapidly. I had the Midas touch in reverse; everything I touched turned to dust.

Sirens were going off somewhere in the distance on the morning of 12 April 1981 as I made my way down to my flat's bathroom. By then we had moved to Surrey Docks, near the Thames, right before it curves around to the Isle of Dogs.

I looked out the window and could see smoke rising from a ways off, coming from Brixton, where a riot had broken out. While we had been partying the night before, a group of young black men had been clashing violently with police, tossing Molotov cocktails at police cars and setting several buildings ablaze. Tensions had been brewing in Brixton over what were known as the "sus" laws, which police had used to stop and question young black men at will. From our flat on the sixth floor, I could see London burning.

A siren was going off in my head as well. My head was splitting with pain from yet another hangover as I made my way past the debris of the previous night's party, sleeping bodies in various states of undress strewn along with empty bottles on the floor. Everyone was still out of it.

What am I doing in this place? I wondered as I picked my way through the bodies and the debris. Once I got to the bathroom, I looked in the mirror at my bloodshot eyes, spiked and scarlet hair, earrings, makeup, nail varnish, my blue jeans covered in safety pins and other punk paraphernalia and said, to no one in particular, "Oh, God, there has to be more to life than this."

I wasn't praying; I was blaspheming, using "Oh, God" as if it were an ordinary expletive. But it was then that a voice answered me.

"Go home," it said. "I'll find you a job, and I'll find you a wife." It wasn't an audible voice; the sensation was of an inner voice or impression, and it was like nothing I'd experienced before.

My ideas of God were a hodgepodge, a combination of Wicca, tarot, transcendental meditation (TM) and Buddhism, all of which I cobbled into a do-it-yourself sort of religion. Throw in a bit of reincarnation, because it meant you could mess up in this life and come back for another one. Mix in a little TM for stress, tarot cards for knowing the future and some Wicca to enchant things around me, and I'd built literally a supermarket of faith. But none of these prepared me for the experience of hearing a voice tell me to go home.

I wasn't keen on the message either. I needed a job but wasn't interested in going home to work in Scarborough. And a wife was definitely not on the agenda. There had been more than enough girls in London to fulfil my every desire. Most of my relationships in London had been very short-term affairs, which suited me just fine. Or so I told myself.

In reality, I was tired of the life I'd been leading, and the rock and roll, booze and bands started to become tedious. I was weary of the fair-weather friends, and I was broke as well. I had become so obnoxious that I had even scared away my best mate at the time; my relationship with him had gone from brother-hood to treachery in the space of a mere few days.

Even though record plugging was a lucrative profession, all of the money I made had gone up, sometimes literally, in smoke. At twenty-two, I was lonely, confused and an emotional wreck. The whole scene in London had lost its appeal, and I didn't want to be a part of it anymore.

Something about this voice seemed too strong to ignore, and within a week, my bags were packed. I gave away all of my albums; since I worked in the record industry, they'd been free anyway. Anything that wouldn't fit in my suitcase I left behind: my TV, most of my clothes, my books and my furniture. I just wanted to get rid of it all and find someplace else where I could start again.

So on a Saturday in late April 1981, I gathered up my suit-case and walked down the stairs from my room in the flat for the last time. There were no tearful goodbyes. I'm not even sure that it registered with anyone in the flat that I was leaving. There'd been a party, as usual, the night before, and my flat-mates were still out cold.

"Right," I called out to no one in particular. "I'm off."

The bus for York left at one o'clock from the Victoria coach station. From York, I could catch a bus home to Scarborough, about forty miles east, along the North Yorkshire coast. I rode the tube with my one suitcase on the seat beside me and got off near the stop for the coach station. After leaving the tube stop, I had an encounter that made me even more eager to get out of London.

As I walked towards Victoria Station, a black man approached from the other direction. When we passed, my suitcase swung around and accidentally knocked into him. It was completely unintentional, but before I could explain, he had turned round and was swearing at me. He shouted, "Get out of here! Get out! Get out!" I thought he was going to beat me up. But after a few more curses and a menacing stare, he stormed off. A great deal of tension was still around at that time – it was a week after the Brixton riots, and people were very angry. It was as if I was being told to keep away from London, and the strangeness of the encounter stuck in my heart like an arrow.

As I boarded the bus for Scarborough, I started to have second thoughts. For a split second, I started to turn around, thinking that I was making a terrible mistake. *Graham, you should just turn around and go back down and try again*, my guts were telling me. But I didn't want to go back. Nothing was left for me in London. I just wanted to get as far away from there as I could.

For most of the journey home, I wondered what I would do with the rest of my life. It felt like I was dying and taking a bus to some other world, and I had no idea of what lay ahead. I was frightened and ashamed that I'd failed, coming home with just ten pounds in my pocket instead of a fortune.

I was somewhat apprehensive about what my parents might say when I arrived home. We hadn't spoken in months. The last time I'd been home was for Christmas, when I'd shown up with a bagful of dirty laundry, hung around for a few days and gone back to London.

I switched buses in York and finally arrived in Scarborough by about seven o'clock. Since no one knew I was coming, I walked home. The bus dropped me off in front of the Scarborough railway station, and from there, I walked past the Stephen Joseph Theatre on Westborough towards Northway, turned along the Columbus Ravine, cut through Peasholm Park and its duck and swan ponds to North Leas Avenue and finally to Maple Drive. Our house was number 94. I walked straight in the door and found my mum in the kitchen.

"Mum, I've come home," I said. "I've had it. I'm not going back to London."

My mum was standing by the sink. She looked at me for a moment and then said, "What took you so long?"

No one killed the fatted calf, but it was a bit like the prodigal son returning home. Mum was pleased to have me back. Nothing was really said about what I had done before, and nothing was held against me.

It was then that I realised what my parents were really like. I had dreaded coming back, dreaded being humiliated. I had talked up so much what I would do in London, lied about my success and romanced about my fortunes. But they took me in and helped me out without a single word of condemnation. It added to my guilt, but I was thankful for it.

5

A Job and a Wife

Even with only one eye, I could still tell she was beautiful. Tall with short brown hair, dressed in jeans and a brown leather jacket, the girl standing by the reception desk at Elder Street Drop-In Centre took my breath away.

I put on my best smile as I walked to the front door, hoping that would compensate for the black patch over my left eye. I had injured my eye the past week, and the patch was doctor's orders. Just my luck, to meet the girl of my dreams while looking like I just stepped out of the pages of *Treasure Island*.

"Is this a new volunteer?" I asked, trying my best to be charming.

Kathy explained that she was just filling out the form, as she'd been told that the centre didn't need any more volunteers at the moment. As the volunteer manager for the centre, I already knew that, but I didn't want to let her get away too quickly.

"Well, would you like to see the building while you're here?" I asked her. "I could show you around – it's no trouble."

As we got in the lift, she turned and looked at me a few times, as if she was trying to figure something out. I made small talk during the tour, trying to impress her with my charm and find out more about her. She'd been on the police force for two and a half years but had soured on police work after the

Yorkshire Ripper case, which had terrorized this part of the country in the late 1970s and early 1980s. She was sick of the violence and wanted to do something that would heal people, so she had started training as a nurse. She was looking for a volunteer job to fill some of her free time and had been making the rounds of all the volunteer organizations in Scarborough.

But everywhere she went, she was told the same thing – they already had sufficient volunteers but would take her name and address and let her know. She was beginning to get a bit desperate, and the Elder Street centre was her last port of call. She hoped the situation would be different since it was a fairly new centre, built to give seniors and people with handicaps a place to go during the day.

I gave her the longest new-volunteer tour ever. We went over the building in great detail – the recreation rooms, kitchen, offices and any other place that I could think of to extend our time. Once we were done, I asked if she had any questions for me.

"Just one," she said, a slightly embarrassed grin creeping across her face. "I don't mean to be rude, but do you have an eye under there?"

Much later, Kathy told me that she knew I was the person she would marry from that first moment. But she wasn't sure she could spend the rest of her life with a one-eyed man, so she had to ask.

I assured her that I did, and we had a laugh. As I let her go, I told her I'd be in touch.

Before long, Kathy had both the volunteer job and me.

God certainly does what he says he will do. I had found the promised job at the centre eighteen months earlier, through a girlfriend who worked there. She asked me if I'd like to come by, as they needed volunteers to spend time with people who had learning disabilities. She knew that my dad was deaf and that I was fluent in sign language and thought I'd be a good match. Soon I began volunteering.

I must have done something right. Towards the end of the summer of 1981, one of the managers approached me and mentioned that a job as an organizer was opening up. "Why don't you apply for it?" she asked, inferring that if I wanted it, the job was mine.

My options at the time were slim; since returning to Scarborough, I hadn't found any other permanent jobs. I figured, why not give social work a go? It couldn't be worse than record plugging.

Being an organizer at the drop-in centre was like being a holiday-camp counsellor for seniors. Mostly it involved planning and running activities. We had bingo sessions and organized coach trips to places of interest. We went to Lincoln, Richmond, York – any place within a two-hour radius. We brought in two professional dancers to run tea dances, which would draw as many as 150 people.

We served tea and coffee and meals, but the main attraction of the centre was social interaction. For most of the people, the centre was the highlight of their week, as they might not have been out of the house or have talked to or been touched by another person in days. While volunteering, I learned that when people get older, they are often deprived of human relationships. Thus, our whole purpose was to help people build friendships.

When Charles, who was in his eighties, first came to the centre, he would sit alone, drinking his tea and not getting involved with others. After a few weeks, some of the other men started talking to him. Before long, he had friends to spend time with as they invited him out to the pub or to the cricket pitch. We measured success by the friendships we helped to form and considered it a job well done when people were so busy on their own – going to lunch, for walks or to the cinema – that they no longer had time to come to the centre.

I was once even asked to be the best man of a couple who met at the centre. They were both in their sixties, and the man had just moved to the area and had no friends nearby. So he asked me to be the best man at their wedding, which was held at the local Baptist church.

I quickly started to feel that this work wasn't bad; I enjoyed serving and helping people. Becoming a social worker was more circumstance than anything else; I didn't go into it out of an altruistic impulse. It was a case of taking the job because there weren't any other options. I took it more for my benefit, because it was helping me and giving me something to do while letting me pay my bills.

But working at the centre taught me a lot about people and made me realise that God had a plan for my life. I became fascinated with life stories. Everyone I met at the centre had really lived. Age seemed a virtue, grey hair an asset.

While working at the centre, I learned a valuable lesson: good deeds are not always rewarded. Soon after returning home, I acquired a cat named Tigger. He was enormous; even as a kitten, he was the size of a small dog. With ginger-and-white-striped fur, Tigger looked more like a miniature lion than a house cat. While he was friendly with humans – to this day, I've never met a more affectionate cat – he hated other animals. Tigger's favourite pastime was roaming the back garden and killing off and eating as many rabbits as he could.

Some friends of mine fell in love with Tigger the first time they saw him. "That's the most fantastic cat I've ever seen," my mate would say whenever he saw Tigger. His girlfriend would beam whenever Tigger would curl up in her lap and purr loudly.

When my friends announced they would be getting married, I knew precisely what to give them as a wedding gift. When they returned from their honeymoon, I presented them with Tigger. They were ecstatic.

Just a week later, however, my mate appeared at my parents' front door, with a cardboard box in hand. "Here's your stupid cat," he said.

My friend had neglected to mention that he had one other pet – a parrot that he kept on a stand in his flat. The parrot used to jump off the stand, circle around the room several times and then settle back down on the stand.

After watching the parrot for several days, Tigger lay in wait for him. As soon as the parrot swooped down close to the floor, Tigger leapt up, and that was that. My friends came home to the sight of Tigger feasting on their pet parrot.

My friend stormed off, and Tigger went back to happily eating rabbits in the back garden. Later I learned that the parrot had cost something like five hundred pounds.

In Scarborough, unlike in London, I'd made some friends who cared deeply about what was happening in my life. One of them was Howard, a colleague at the Elder Street centre. When I started working at the centre, I learned very early on that he was a Christian, as were many of my colleagues. God has got this sneaky way of surrounding you with Christians if he is trying to get your attention. If you don't watch it, they'll start praying for you, and your life will never be the same.

Howard in particular impressed me with his kindness. He was married to an old friend of mine from school, Rachel, with whom I started school when we were six or seven years old. I sometimes went over to Howard and Rachel's house for dinner or spent an evening out with them. They had a kind of peace or contentment in life that I didn't have.

The more time I spent with Howard, the more I began to rethink some of my assumptions about the Christian faith. I'd always thought that church was boring, irrelevant and untrue, that it was full of people who didn't really believe what Jesus taught. I'd always liked Jesus and thought he was a good man. Over the years, no matter what kind of scrapes I got in, I always felt there was something important about this Jesus figure. Even when I was practicing Wicca, I would pray to Jesus. I must be the biggest failure of a witch ever, because whenever I would cast a spell or try to curse someone, the word "Jesus" kept coming into my head and distracting me.

My friendship with Howard and Rachel also revealed to me what a total and absolute mess my life was. I was promiscuous, a liar, a cheat and a drunk. One of the reasons I'd done so well at record plugging was that the lies would just roll off my tongue, almost without effort. Most of the time I thought solely of my own satisfaction. If getting something I wanted meant betraying or hurting someone else, I would do it easily. I felt dirty, as if my actions had spattered my being with grime and muck.

Life was all about me. And I was miserable.

The thing was, there seemed to be no hope of changing my life. I'd tried looking into every religion I could think of, and none had helped. Wicca hadn't brought me happiness. I read about Islam and found I could never measure up to the demands of the Koran. Buddhism was even worse, for if I lived by the law of karma – which says that what you do in this life affects what happens in your next life – there would be no hope for me. Even if I completely changed directions and lived to be a hundred, I'd done so much wrong by the age of twenty-two that I could never make up for it. I was doomed to come back in the next life as a slug.

I remember explaining this all to Howard one day when we should have been working. "Look, Howard," I said, "I've done things in my life that I really regret doing, and I've been a person I really regret being. And now I am stuck. There is no way I can get rid of these things I've done."

Howard listened to me intently and then said in a kind voice, "Of course there is. Of course there's a way you can be rid of these things."

Then he quoted me something from the Bible, a passage he knew by heart: "If we claim to be without sin, we deceive ourselves and the truth is not in us. But if we confess our sins, God is faithful and just and will forgive us our sins and purify us from all unrighteousness" (1 John 1:8–9).

When I asked Howard what exactly that "purify us from all unrighteousness" bit meant, he said, "Look, you've made a mess of your life. You know it, I know it and God knows it. You need to start over. And if you ask God to help you, he will. It will be as if God brings a curtain down on your life. What is in the past is forgiven and forgotten; what is in the future is brand new."

A few weeks later, I was having a similar discussion with another friend from the centre, a guy called Simon. Simon was much like Howard – very serious about his faith and really kind to me. We were walking home at the end of the day, and I was telling him about the mess I'd found myself in.

He told me that if I asked Jesus to get me out of this mess, he would. As we were talking, we came to the place where our paths split, outside a store called Spa.

"Look," he said, "you've got to decide one way or the other. You either accept Jesus as your Saviour or continue walking your own way. It's no good sitting on the fence."

Going my way wasn't very appealing, so right then and there, I looked up to the heavens and said, "Lord Jesus, if you are out there, please come into my life."

Nothing happened. No flashing lights, no voice from heaven, no road-to-Damascus experience. Just Simon and I standing outside the Spa shop, talking to God.

It was much like what C. S. Lewis described in his autobiography, *Surprised by Joy*: "I gave in, and admitted that God was God, and knelt and prayed: perhaps that night, the most dejected and reluctant convert in all England." I was a similarly reluctant convert. I didn't experience any overwhelming emotions or spiritual fireworks. I needed help, so I turned to God.

Soon afterwards, my life began to change in small ways. I started going to church, which was a huge step because it meant I had to get over my problems with church. I had a preconceived notion that Christians were like manure: when they're spread thinly, they're fine; but get a bunch together, and they stink. I thought church would be full of holier-than-thou Christians.

When I started going to church, I found the people were warm and friendly, but the services were just as bad as I thought they would be. The songs were terrible, and the sermons were boring. But I kept going. Because I had made a commitment to God, I had also decided I would worship with other Christians on Sundays. So week after week, I went to church, and the more I went, the more faith began to rub off on me and change my personality.

Church became a good place to be. I found a family of people prepared to share their lives. When I listened to the words of the hymns, they started to make me break down in tears. I realised it was Jesus that I needed, and only him. I was finally being made whole, set free from all that had come upon my life in the past.

I also started going to a Bible study group, where people get together at someone's house to read the Bible and talk about it together. There I realised that these Christians were normal people. But early on, I felt embarrassed because I didn't fully understand what they were talking about. I hated being in that situation, so I would pretend I knew what they meant. But I was certain of one thing: the Son of God loved me and cared about me, and because of that, I could make a new start in my life.

God wants to be part of our lives. No matter how far we've fallen away from him, no matter how good or bad we are, he is still prepared to reach down to us. Christians call it grace – God's overwhelming kindness and willingness to be deeply involved in the life of a very weak and very poor person like me. Grace means getting something you don't deserve: a second chance at life.

For someone like me, who was an utter mess, grace became a lifesaver. I absolutely believe that if I hadn't become a Christian, I'd be dead today. God gave me something to live for. Otherwise, the temptations of the world would have been too strong. I'd have ended up dying alone and forgotten, at far too young an age.

Ever since that moment in front of the Spa shop, my life began to change very slowly and gradually. It took many years for God to sort me out – to clean out all of the rubbish that I'd filled my life with. But since that time, God has completely transformed me. I still have a long ways to go, and I am far from perfect, but together with God I am going somewhere.

My conversion experience taught me that no one is beyond saving. If God could straighten out the mess I'd made of my life, he can do it for anyone. Some people think that God cares only about people who are holy or who are good and respectable. But the Christian faith is about a God who died to save us when we didn't deserve it. When Jesus died on the cross, he made amends for me, because I couldn't do it for myself.

I know that God loves me no matter what state I'm in. Because I'm a human being, my relationship with God has ups and downs, good days and bad days. Sometimes I feel close to God and deeply spiritual, but other times I feel very far away from him; I don't feel very Christian or holy or anything like that. Yet God is still there and loves me. He is constant, and I can depend on that.

The voice that spoke to me in London promised me a job, and it also promised me a wife. The wife took a little longer, as I had been living in Scarborough for more than a year and a half before Kathy and I first met.

At the time, Kathy was living with two of her friends at her parents' house while they were in Istanbul. After our first encounter at Elder Street, she went home and told her friends that they needed to go out and celebrate. "I've met the man I'm going to marry," she told them.

She had no doubt in her mind. And neither did I – one who had never believed in love at first sight, or really even in love itself. But now I had met someone who I just knew was the person for me. When I first saw Kathy, those words from London – "I'll find you a wife" – popped into my head.

Things were complicated on my end. I knew from that first moment that Kathy was the woman I wanted to marry, but I was seeing someone else, a girl named Peg. I didn't want a repeat of situations in which I had cheated on people, but I didn't want to be cruel to the girl I was with and just dump her for someone I hardly knew. But I didn't want to let Kathy get away either. So for a while I saw both of them.

The dates with Kathy were different from any I'd ever had. For one thing, they were platonic; that in itself was a big change. We spent our time walking and talking and getting to know each other as friends. It was a novel idea.

Kathy and I met in December of 1982, and by January, I knew without a doubt that she was the one. So I had to come clean with the other woman I was seeing. We were at Peg's house on a Saturday night and were sitting on the couch, talking. All the while I was wishing I was with Kathy instead. For the first time, I felt guilty about the way I was behaving. It wasn't fair for me to be spending my free time with Kathy, even if we weren't romantically involved.

Ever the blunt person, I blurted out the truth. "Look, I'm sorry, but I've met someone else. I don't want to cheat on you, so we'll have to break things off."

With that, I got up and walked right out Peg's house, waving goodbye as I went out the door. From there, I went straight to Kathy's house and asked her to marry me. She said yes, and three days later, I moved in and her friends moved out. I was still new in my Christian faith and hadn't realised that living together was out of bounds. In my eyes, it seemed perfectly fine because Kathy was the person I was going to marry.

When I started living with Kathy, I finally began to eat like a normal person. Before meeting her, my diet consisted of four pints of beer a day and a couple of packets of rye crisps. Like I said, God had a lot of work to do to straighten me out. At the time, I weighed about ten or eleven stone (about 150 pounds), even though I was six feet one, with a twenty-eight-inch waist.

When I lived in London, along with all my other bingeing, I binged on food. I'd overeat, starve myself for a few days and then stuff myself again. That's why I don't have any photographs of me from that time; I didn't want to let anyone take my picture. No matter how skinny I became, I always thought I needed to lose more weight. I can trace it back to being a fat child and other kids at school calling me "Porky." From that moment on, to avoid being bullied for being a fatty, I started to diet and diet and diet.

A few weeks after moving in with Kathy, I got dreadfully ill with the flu – so sick that I began to hallucinate. She nursed me through that time. When I recovered, she started feeding me soup and then regular food. The more the food came, the more I piled on the weight and began to look like a normal human being.

Kathy and I were engaged in early January and were married 23 July 1983, seven months after we met. The Reverend Chris Tubbs married us at St Laurence's Church in Scalby. I was twenty-four; Kathy was twenty-two.

It was a typical fairy-book wedding. The tyre went flat on the taxi on the way to the reception, and the driver had to change it while Kathy was waiting inside. Then there were all the usual hassles that go along with planning a wedding. We worried more about the seating arrangements – who was going to be next to whom at the reception – than about the actual idea of getting married. The wedding itself went off without a hitch, with our families there to celebrate with us.

Most of the day was a blur. The great thing was getting out of the reception at about eleven o'clock at night and heading back to the hotel so we could finally have some time alone. There, at the Royal Hotel in Scarborough, Kathy and I shared our first meal as husband and wife – sandwiches and rye crisps, washed down with a bottle of champagne. It was brilliant, and so were the sandwiches. We had started on the grand adventure of marriage.

We took our honeymoon in late September, hiring a boat for a couple of weeks while cruising the Norfolk Broads, a large fenland area in eastern England. When we arrived to get the boat, I should have been suspicious, as I could see that the guy showing us around had obviously been on a high-maintenance, hard-cider habit for a number of years. He gleefully showed us how to steer the boat while making all the usual jokes about newlyweds. In parting, he told us to take it steady.

Kathy and I set off, looking forward to enjoying some time alone and planning for the future. As we majestically cruised along the canal, I surveyed the scene. Fishermen puffed on pipes of tobacco as water birds scooted from our path. Kathy was cooking away below deck, preparing tea and cake, as the sun began to set.

"Would you like to steer?" I asked as Kathy came on deck and handed me a mug of tea. She smiled and took control, turning slightly as I put my arm around her and kissed her cheek. All of a sudden the boat accelerated violently, lurching from side to side as the rudder flapped this way and that. Tea went flying as the boat literally spun in the water before crashing against the side of the canal and launching an unsuspecting fisherman into the water. What seemed like yards of steering cable whooshed from some hidden place as the snapped cable unwound itself from the wheel. The boat eventually came to rest on a far bank as we heard the distant shouting of the soaked fisherman.

Within minutes of reporting the accident, the man from the boatyard appeared with his mate, who was drunker than he was. Together they rummaged below deck and soon assured us that all was now well.

"Slight technical hitch," one of them said as they staggered back into the small speedboat they had arrived in and sped off into the night.

That night we slept fitfully. The boat was cold, it leaked, the windows wouldn't close, and the countryside was noisy. Ducks quacked, cows moaned, owls hooted, and revellers at the nearby pub sang "I am sailing . . ." over and over as they pretended to be Rod Stewart. The next morning we woke up early, roused from sleep by the mooing of the cows in the fields along the shore. Kathy slipped into the shower as I set sail for Ranworth Broad, a large expanse of open water. I could hear the shower pump churning away; I could also hear Kathy moaning that there was no water. I told her that I could hear the water running and all would be well. Again moans, and again replies not to worry.

But I was the first to worry when I looked below deck and saw water bubbling up from beneath the carpets. In his inso-briety, the drunken deckhand had knocked the outflow pipe off the water tank. So as Kathy waited for the water, it was pumped into the bilges at such a pace that it filled the boat.

Kathy appeared from the shower, covered in shampoo. I hur-riedly aimed the watercraft for the bank and told her to put on her lifebelt.

In the days before mobile phones, stranded sailors had to walk for help. The boat had come to rest in the middle of nowhere, so I set off on foot to get help, heading for a church steeple I could see, some miles away. I had tied the boat to the bank with a rond anchor and left Kathy to fend for herself.

I could hear the engine of a far-off tractor. Seeing it in the distance, I set off towards it in the hope that the farmer could take me to the boatyard. At that point, I slipped into a muddy dyke, only to reappear like a swamp monster from the depths. I ran on across the fields, squelching with mud and looking as if I was a madman. For that, I truly was.

I waved frantically at the farmer, who was ploughing away. I knew I had caught his eye by the alarmed look on his face and by the fact that he pulled the plough from the ground, turned quickly and sped off. Not to be outdone, I gave chase across the burnt stubble. He drove even faster. From what I could see, I realised that if I took another shortcut, I could beat him to the road. I desperately wanted a lift, and he wasn't going to get away. I jumped the fence and fell into yet another dyke. I ran across the field and, just as the farmer thought he had made an escape, launched myself into the lane in front of his vehicle. He stopped, locked the cab door and stared at me.

"Help?" I muttered, unsure what to say.

Within the hour, the farmer rather reluctantly took me to the boatyard. Throughout the journey, he eyed me warily and never spoke.

Eventually the two drunken mechanics pumped out the boat and fixed the engine, and we were again on our way. Having watched what they had done, I decided to adapt the engine and take off the speed restricter. The ship had never gone so fast and never was a bow wave so big on the Norfolk Broads.

Some hours later, we docked at a sleepy harbour that had a great pub at which to eat. Our plates of fish and chips arrived promptly, and we were looking forward to tucking in. Just then two spaniel dogs rushed in. They jumped on our table, knocked our food to the floor, ate it and ran out again.

The next day, things only got worse. Sitting in a beer garden at a waterside pub, Kathy and I looked at each other dreamily. The place was packed with families, couples and children, all eating in the autumn sun. It was then that Kathy suddenly grasped her neck and began to scream like a banshee. The man to my right let out a shout of concern, believing I had struck this poor woman.

"It's my wife ..." I said just above the sound of Kathy's screaming. I tried to take hold of her to see what was wrong. All Kathy could do was hold her neck and scream even louder through floods of tears.

"What's wrong?" I asked as the whole beer garden came to her aid and looked at me as if I were an abusive husband.

"Wasp ... wasp ..." she replied woefully, holding her hands to her neck, where a lump from the sting grew like a boil in need of lancing.

All in all, the honeymoon was much like our wedding – something out of a fairy book. Despite the best efforts of drunken boatyard workers, spaniel dogs and an angry wasp, it was brilliant. And the adventure was just beginning.

6

Plastic Couch and Poltergeist

The noise sounded like footsteps, as if someone or something were coming down the stairs. But aside from Kathy and me, along with our dog, Greta, no one else was in the house.

I looked over as a shade from an upstairs lamp came rolling into the front room, where we were sitting. This had been a recurring problem. Something kept knocking the shade off the lamp and sending it cascading down the stairs. When it got to the bottom, it never rolled to the left into the back room, but always to the right into the front room. Once again, I carried the shade back up to the lamp. This time I tied a length of fuse wire to it to keep it in place.

Problem solved, I thought. But a few days later, the shade came bouncing down the steps again. We'd had a number of strange problems like this ever since we moved into a snug cottage in Scalby, a village just on the outskirts of Scarborough, in 1984. We fell in love with the house the first time we saw it, nestled in a row of terraced cottages along the main street. So with the help of a 99 percent mortgage, we bought it for £17,000, using money we'd saved by living in Kathy's parents' house during our first year of marriage.

Within a week of moving in, odd things began to happen. The taps would suddenly go on and off by themselves, but when the plumber came out, he found nothing wrong with the pipes. Doors would slam when no one was near them. Money could go missing, as would clothes; we'd set them down and later find them moved to another spot. Little things, but they were unnerving.

Then one Saturday, I was working in the back garden when I heard some banging coming from the upstairs window. I looked up and saw a man standing in the upstairs bedroom, wearing a white shirt with rolled-up sleeves and dark trousers. Dropping the gardening tools, I ran inside, taking the stairs two at time. But when I opened the door to the bedroom, he had vanished.

Because of my experiences with the occult, I was frightened that some kind of ghost or poltergeist was in the house. It was more than just the rolling lampshade and the appearance of a man in the window; we had an overwhelming sense that we were being watched. Greta, our dog, felt it too. Sometimes she would sit at the bottom at the stairs and growl, then show her teeth and lunge at something we couldn't see.

One day while I was at work, Kathy had another disturbing encounter. Though neither Kathy nor I were handy, we had decided to fix up the cottage, as it had fallen into a bad state of disrepair and was old, having been built in 1887. The wallpaper was dark and battered and gave the house a dismal feeling, so Kathy was covering it with some off-white paint. She was standing on a ladder and reaching towards the ceiling when all of a sudden the temperature in the room dropped markedly. It was the middle of summer, but inside the house, it felt like the middle of winter. She felt a wave of dread come over her, like something malevolent was in the room with her.

Kathy, an ex-copper, does not frighten easily. She got off the ladder and went downstairs, trying to convince herself that she was just imagining things. *This is the 1980s*, she told herself, *and things like this just don't happen*. But when she went back up and started to paint again, she felt the same things – a dreadful cold and the sense that something was trying to get her. She was so frightened that she refused to go back upstairs until I came home.

Things went on like this for about ten months. While Kathy was at work, I slept downstairs on the couch, not wanting to be upstairs at night. Looking back, it sounds funny, but we had a physical sense of something malevolent in the house. I kept hoping that if we ignored the problem, it would go away. But it didn't.

We were going to St Laurence's Church in Scalby at the time, and out of desperation, I went to see Chris Tubbs, the vicar who had married us. He listened to my story, thought it over for a minute or so and then gave some straightforward advice: "Go into your house and pray and tell whatever it is to go in the name of Jesus."

"If that doesn't work," he said as I left, "come and get me."

When I got home, I told Kathy what Chris had said. So we gave it a try. We prayed the Lord's Prayer, the prayer that Jesus taught his disciples, and then we told the spirit or poltergeist, or whatever it was, that it had to go. On paper, this sounds more spiritual than it was in real life. What actually happened was more like this: we said the Lord's Prayer, and then I screamed at the top of my lungs, "In the name of Jesus, leave this place."

We must have done something right because all of the strange happenings came to an end. We could finally enjoy our new home.

Interestingly, some years later, after I'd written about this incident in one of the London papers, one of our former neighbours from Jubilee Terrace contacted me. She'd experienced many of the same odd happenings that we had, and they'd disappeared from her house about the same time they'd disappeared from ours.

Before moving to the cottage, we had never really prayed before, but we found ourselves praying almost every day once we moved in. We needed all the help we could get. As I mentioned earlier, the house needed a great deal of work, and neither one of us was very handy.

Our first project was the kitchen, which was a tiny room that held only a sink and a very old cooker that somebody had left in the house. In the back of the kitchen were two doors that opened into coal sheds. We didn't need coal sheds inside the house, so we decided to knock out the wall and open up the kitchen to have more space. We really had no clue what we were doing.

Before we could make too much of a wreck of things, our dear friend Stephen Clarkson came to our rescue. He was a plasterer by trade and helped us knock the wall down. When we were done, the kitchen was roomier, though still very rough. The floor wasn't level where the wall had been, so there was a great lump underneath the linoleum. Looking back, it was pretty awful.

Our other major challenge was money. We were quite poor in those days. The cottage had cost us £17,000, and all of my salary from Elder Street went to pay the mortgage. Kathy's nursing salary went towards all our other necessities and any home-repair projects, leaving little left over for luxuries like furniture or curtains. We had a bed and a kitchen table and chairs but little else.

Some friends from the deaf club in town took pity on us, and when the club replaced their curtains, they let us have the old ones. When we first got them, we thought the curtains were white. But when we unfolded them, we discovered they were actually green and white striped. They had been in the sun so long that they had faded to white except where the folds had been. They were so faded that they'd actually started splitting down the fades because the fabric was so old and frayed. But faded curtains were better than no curtains, and we were grateful.

"Ask and it shall be given to you," Jesus once said. We needed a couch, so I decided to ask God for one.

Kathy and I had been sitting on the floor, going round and round about how we could get a couch. We couldn't afford one and didn't know anyone who was getting rid of an old one. The thought just popped into my head. "I'm sure God would give us a couch if we asked for one," I told Kathy.

Kathy thought I was bonkers. "We are not asking God for a couch," she said incredulously. To her, the idea was out of the question.

"Why not?" I asked. "I've been reading in the Bible that God says he will take care of our needs. We need a couch, so why not ask God for one?"

"It's a bit cheeky, don't you think, asking God for a couch?" she responded.

For the next hour, we sat there arguing about whether or not we could ask God for a couch. Eventually Kathy gave in. Since the Book of Common Prayer doesn't exactly have a section on prayers for a new couch, we made up one of our own.

Kathy started praying, still a little bit nervous but explaining to God our current lack of living-room furniture. "If this is making you a bit cross, us asking for a couch, please forgive us, but we do actually need one," she prayed. "It's a bit embarrassing when people come in and they have to sit on the floor. We don't even have a cushion on the floor or anything."

We went on like this for a few minutes, and then at the end, I added this caveat: "Lord, if you do send us a couch, please don't send us a white plastic one. I can't stand them. I do not want a white plastic couch."

"That was a bit rude," Kathy said once the prayer was over.

Here I was asking God for a couch and then getting picky about it. But I wanted to make sure God knew what I had in mind.

The next day at work, a woman came into the Elder Street centre, asking to see me.

"I was thinking about you last night," she said. "You've just bought a new house, haven't you?"

"That's right," I answered.

"Do you have any furniture?" she said.

"Well, not a lot," I admitted. "Why do you ask?"

"We've just bought a new suite," she said, "and it arrived today, so we need to get our old one out. It is just one sofa, that's all, but if you want it, it's yours."

This woman lived in a very nice part of Scarborough, so images of a stunning leather sofa popped into my head. Thanking her for the offer, I told her that we'd come by that night and get it. As soon as she walked out the door, I started rubbing my hands together, already anticipating our good fortune. God, it seemed, had heard our prayer and had come through for us.

Howard had a Land Rover and offered to help me get the couch. He picked me up after tea, and on the drive over, I started telling him the story of how we'd prayed for this couch, how God had provided a fine leather sofa for us, and how great it all was. I even told him the line about no plastic couches.

"Be careful what you pray for, Graham," he said. "God's got a wicked sense of humour."

"No way," I told Howard. "It's going to be a leather sofa."

We drove down the beautiful tree-lined avenue where the woman lived and parked outside her house. When we got inside, the new suite was sitting in the middle of the room. It was an absolutely stunning, gorgeous leather suite. *I knew it,* I thought to myself. I just knew her old one was going to be leather.

"We've put the old couch in the back room, Graham," she said.

I went in, then took a deep breath as I looked at the largest, whitest, most plastic couch I'd ever seen in my life. I couldn't believe it. Howard just smiled at me.

When we got back to the cottage with the couch, Kathy just stood there with her mouth open as we carried it in, barely able to suppress her laughter.

We all sat down on our new couch for a cup of tea with Howard, who graciously had not said anything about its being plastic. About half an hour later, we heard a car drive up. As the cottage was set up about five feet above the level of the road, we could see the tops of cars as they drove by. Looking out the window, we caught sight of an immense, black plastic couch.

A minute later, my friend Paul was at the door, a wide smile on his face.

"Graham," he said, "we knew you needed a couch and look what we've found for you!"

At this point, Kathy was on the floor, keeled over with laughter.

So in the space of twenty-four hours after praying to God, we were the proud new owners of a white plastic couch and a black plastic couch. As I thought about it, I started to worry. Would God now be sending us a big, green plastic couch and a big, red plastic couch and then every colour plastic couch one could imagine?

The funniest thing was that the white couch was very comfy. Once I sat on it, I hardly ever wanted to get off. I learned two lessons that day. One was to be careful what I asked God for, because Howard was right – God's got an amazing sense of humour. The other was to leave the details to God. If we get exactly what we want, there's no room for God to surprise us. We experienced God's providence – he *would* care for our needs.

We settled into a routine over the next few years. I worked during the days at the drop-in centre, while Kathy worked overnight shifts at the hospital. On Sundays, we would go to church together, and we began running the youth club at St Laurence's a few evenings a week.

I enjoyed being involved with the teenagers at the youth club. It was my first chance to talk about what God had done in my life. I told them about my years in London, the drinking and the drugs, and how absolutely miserable I had been until I came to know God.

Working with the youth club prodded me to think about the future. Was I going to remain where I was, doing social work and volunteering at church, or would I pursue a different direction? One night after youth club, Chris asked me if I thought God was calling me to ministry. I told him I'd been considering it.

Soon afterwards I started praying with Chris and a couple of other people every day after work. We'd meet at church at half past five and pray together for half an hour. The more we met for prayer, the more I became convinced that God was calling me to this way of life. So Chris put me in touch with the director of ordinands, the person who organizes the training for ministers for the diocese of York, and he sent me to a local fellowship group for those considering ordination.

Since I'd been expelled from sixth form college and had never been to university, I wasn't sure if I would be accepted. But the Church of England's ordination scheme has an exception for people like me. I had to get permission to take the courses, which were graduate level. They must have seen some promise in me, as I was accepted to begin the training process.

At that time, my biggest influences were my local priest and the verger, a man named Ken who was a fine, tall man, always impeccably dressed and always ready to go the extra mile. As we prayed together every evening, it became the most important part of the day for me.

One winter evening, I learned that both the vicar and Ken would be away the following evening and that I should say evensong alone. I felt really honoured to be trusted to come into the church and read the psalms. As it was just getting dark, I entered the old church and could hear the wind whistling through the trees outside. I left the door ajar to give extra light, as I couldn't find the light switches. In the half dark, I began to pray by candlelight and read the Scriptures. The reading was from Luke: "I saw Satan fall like lightening from the sky ..." On cue, it happened – the first roll of thunder from the hills.

I held my breath, looked around the empty church and closed my eyes to say the intercessions. I then became aware of the church door slowly opening and the sound of hoofed feet tiptoeing across the floor. I looked in the direction of the sound but could see nothing. The footsteps beat sharply across the stone steps and across the gravel and were gone.

Was this a visit from the horned one (Satan)? I wondered if he had chosen this night to come for my soul. The sound came again, this time joined by another set of cloven feet. *Two devils*, I thought as my mind raced, *and getting closer.* Step by step, they passed behind the back pew.

I said the Lord's Prayer faster and faster, and then there they were – not devils, but goats. The vicar's goats had come to see their absent master. The good shepherd had left me in charge, and his churchyard grass eaters had picked the scariest night of the year to make a holy house call.

"Do you love God more than you love me?" Kathy asked one day as we were sitting on our white plastic couch.

Before answering, I knew that my answer would get me into trouble. "Yes," I responded, looking into her eyes. I've always been a blunt, stick-my-foot-in-it person, and I knew I couldn't beat around the bush in answering this question. Still, I could tell it hurt her. She looked away from me and drew back, not wanting to be next to me.

So I tried a different approach. "Look," I said, "when you die, God is still going to be alive. We could split up, and God is always going to be there for me. My love for God is different from my love for you. I want to love God with all my heart, and if I do that, I'll be able to love you even better."

As you might expect, this made things even worse.

Kathy thought I was being weird. Her road to faith had been different from mine. My life had been a wreck before I became a Christian, so I had a constant sense of gratitude. I was so thankful that God took pity on me and straightened me out. I tried to explain this. "If it wasn't for God, we never would have met or married, and I'd still be living in London, drinking and drugging, stuck in a self-destructive life."

She didn't seem swayed.

"You are a gift from God," I said, hoping that would reassure her that I didn't love her any less.

My explanation didn't convince her, and wouldn't for some time. Perhaps it's better if Kathy explains it in her own words.

> When Graham and I were first married, I was very jealous of God. Because the more I talked to Graham about his faith, the more I realised that he put God first. And I thought, *Well, he's putting somebody else before me,* and it made me feel very insecure.

But God was working in my life. At the time, I was working with a nurse who was a Christian, and she kept leaving me Christian books to read. One was called *God's Smuggler* by a Dutchman named Brother Andrew, a former soldier who smuggled Bibles into Poland and Russia during the cold war.

I don't recall the whole gist of the story, but I remember that he was very honest about how he killed some civilians while fighting with the Dutch army and how that had impacted his life. He later became a Christian and smuggled Bibles into Russia.

I was really into this book, especially when he was teaching teenagers to say what he called the "sinner's prayer." He told the teenagers that if they wanted to know God, all they had to do was ask. He had them say a simple prayer, admitting that they had sinned, that they needed God's help, and then ask Jesus into their lives. That really spoke to me because I thought, *No one's ever told me that, that we can change our relationship with God.* So I knelt down right by my chair and said the sinner's prayer. That was the beginning for me, though I progressed very slowly. In the early days, Graham was much more in tune with his Christian faith than I was.

It wasn't long before my training as a clergyman began to go off the rails. My faith was growing, and I still enjoyed working with the youth club, but the more I was exposed to the hierarchy of the church, the more I began to get concerned. For one thing, I started to see some stuff in the church that I wasn't seeing in the Scripture. The Church of England is an organization that is grey around the edges, and I started to wonder if I would have to compromise to get along. For instance, some people in the church hold the idea that we are saved through our baptism, especially infant baptism. But I couldn't find anywhere in the Scripture where it says that you'll be saved if you get baptized. It says believe and be baptized, not be baptized and believe later on in life.

And many people I was coming across in the church had God-centred ideas about salvation, with Jesus playing a minor role. That is, they would say that they believed in God but had trouble with Jesus. For me, however, Jesus was the most important thing. So I thought I'd have to compromise on that as well.

I thought a lot of indoctrination was going on – where I was expected to go along with things I didn't believe in. Being an evangelical Christian can be embarrassing; you can be seen as some kind of extremist or fundamentalist. I was always telling people that I was sorry for what I believed.

I also saw the backbiting that can go on in church politics. People would tear each other apart with cruel language or go behind each other's backs if it helped their cause. People were talking the talk – going on and on about Jesus or "Christian love" – but weren't walking the walk. The more time I spent in the training courses, the more disenchanted and cynical I became.

After completing the local training courses, the director of ordinands suggested that I go to theological college for a year of full-time study. He gave me several options. The first was to go away for a year at Mirfield, an Anglo-Catholic theological college about a hundred miles away, and the other option was to go to Edinburgh and study there. Both options meant leaving Kathy behind for a year, and that didn't feel right. So in the end, I told the director that I wasn't going anywhere and started to break from the training programme.

I could blame the liberals or the backbiting in the church for making me leave, but that's not the whole truth. The deeper truth is that I was avoiding addressing the growing sense of insecurity I had about becoming a priest. I was a guy from the wrong side of the tracks and thought that people like me had no business being ordained. More important, I was afraid of failing God. I thought that being a minister meant I would be responsible to God for everything I did. I feared that I would fail God and wouldn't be up to the task. I was also afraid that I wasn't up to the job that God had called me to, and wasn't ready to admit it.

So I did a Jonah, meaning the man in the Old Testament who ran in the opposite direction as far as he could and got swallowed by a big fish. For me, instead of becoming a vicar, I became a police officer. I'd never read anything in the Bible about a police officer being called to the ministry. I thought I'd be safe there and not have to listen to God's call.

In one sense, joining the police force was an obvious choice. A number of my friends were constables, and they loved the job. Serving as a police officer also runs in my family. Kathy had been on the force before becoming a nurse, and my grand-father was a policeman for most of his life. Known as "Taller Taylor," he'd been a boxer before joining the force. He was a good fighter and a drinker, which made him an ideal policeman in the 1930s. I inherited the fighting and drinking from him, though I'd given up drinking when I came back from London.

I started training as a police officer in January 1987. My first course was in Thirsk, the village made famous in *All Creatures Great and Small*, where Alfred White (known to the world as James Herriot) had his famed animal surgery. This was fol-lowed by fourteen weeks in Durham at a police training school. I trained in crime, law, riot training, how to diffuse a bomb and all sorts of things.

The final step in the training was the passing-out parade, which was held at the station in Durham. It's an important day; our family and friends came to see us dressed in our best police uniforms, all pressed and immaculate. My dad came up for the parade, and I remember seeing tears in his eyes as he saw me in my uniform, marching down the parade square.

Afterwards, for the first time in years, he came up to me and just hugged me. It was his way of saying that everything was okay now. I was twenty-seven years old and hadn't realised until that moment how much my dad loved me. For years, I had been angry and hostile towards him, never thinking about his needs. I hadn't been a son at all.

But when I saw those tears in my father's eyes on the parade grounds, I knew that he loved me. And that he was proud of me. It was all I needed. He had lived a hard life, he wasn't perfect; none of us are. But in all my time as his son, I had read the guy wrong. I never understood what it must be like to be deaf and live in a hearing world. That day, I slowly began to understand.

7

LIFE IN THE BALANCE

My first posting as a police officer was in Northallerton, a city of about 20,000 people, where I had done most of my training. Getting a permanent assignment meant that Kathy and I would be living together again, as we had spent January to April of 1987 apart while I was in training, seeing each other only on weekends. We moved to Northallerton on the fifteenth of April, having sold our cottage to some friends. Our new home was a semi-detached police house in Northallerton, about one hundred yards from a prison. Every day the inmates would pass our house when they went to work in the city gardens. They knew that a police officer lived there, so they'd hurl curses at us as they walked by, making for interesting breakfast entertainment.

About the same time as our move, we learned that Kathy was pregnant and was due in December. With a new home, a new job and a baby on the way, life seemed very good indeed.

My first year as a police officer was a probationary period to see if I was cut out for the job. I'd done well in the classroom training and field experience, but there's a big difference between being a trainee and being a constable. To help with the transition, I was assigned a tutor constable, who would teach me the practical parts of the job – and keep me out of trouble.

On my first night on the job, I was assigned my call number, 393, which I would keep for the whole of my police career. I dressed in my black constable uniform and helmet, with a radio clipped to my uniform shirt along with my North Yorkshire Police badge. A long, black torch, my truncheon and a set of handcuffs were clipped to my belt.

The shift started at 10:00 p.m., and my tutor and I spent the first few hours walking the beat without incident. So far so good. Then a call came in over the radio – a burglar was in a pub on the high street, not far from where we were. We broke into a fast walk and were on the scene in a couple of minutes.

"I'm going to the front door," my tutor told me. "You check around back."

My tutor's instructions seemed odd; I thought we were supposed to stick together. I hesitated for a moment, thinking of the right way to remind my tutor of this. Nothing came to mind, so I turned quickly and walked towards the alleyway that led behind the pub.

Northallerton is a medieval town, dating back to AD 1200, and has long, narrow alleyways running behind the shops. The alleyway behind the pub was not well lit, and there were plenty of shadows for a burglar to hide in, so I walked slowly at first, casting my torch about and trying to recall the correct procedures for entering a building where an intruder was present.

My radio crackled to life. It was my tutor: "393, we think that the burglar is in the garage. Can you respond?"

I radioed back, telling my tutor that I could handle it. As I got closer to the pub, I doused my torch, hoping to sneak up on the burglar. I walked down the stone path cautiously, with my truncheon in one hand, the torch in the other, trying to make as little noise as possible.

The garage door was open, so I ducked in quickly. The lights were off, and I couldn't see any sign of a burglar. From somewhere in the corner of the garage came the muffled sound of breathing. My heart sped up a few notches. This was my first arrest, and I wanted to be sure not to botch it. I crept a few paces forward, trying to get as close as possible before making my move. The plan was to shine the torch on the burglar's face to disorient him, shout "Police!" in a loud voice and then speedily make the arrest.

The closer I got to the burglar, the more I began to realise that something was not right. I couldn't put my finger on it yet, but I thought the breathing sounded like it was coming from the floor.

That's odd, I thought. *What's the burglar doing down there?*

I took a few more steps. Something rustled in the corner, and then I heard a clink of metal. It was time to act. Aiming my torch towards the corner, I flicked on the switch. The light fell on two red, glowing eyes, staring back at me from the corner of the garage. Just below the eyes was a mouthful of pointy and sharp teeth, glittering in my torchlight. I heard a low, threatening growl as something large and snarling lunged at me. I turned tail and ran for my life. This was not exactly how I imagined starting my police career.

The snarling beast was the biggest Alsatian dog I had ever seen. I ran out of the garage, towards the alleyway. The Alsatian was right behind me, its claws scraping on the stone walkway and its barking thundering in my ears.

From the alley, I heard laughter. My tutor and about six other police officers were standing in the alley; their mouths open in wide grins. I ran past them just as the Alsatian was about to grab hold of my rear end. Suddenly the dog gave a howl and was jerked back. The dog's chain stopped just short of the alley, and I was safe.

My new colleagues had set me up. All the crew from the police station, including the inspector, had turned up, and they were in howling fits of laughter. They knew the dog slept in the garage and that it didn't like people. They certainly got me.

I suppose they would have come to my rescue if the dog had caught me. But I'm not sure – they were laughing too hard.

A few days later, my sergeant sent me for another initiation ceremony, this time at the mortuary. An older gentleman had died following surgery at a local hospital, and the coroner was performing a postmortem. In England, laws require a postmortem if someone dies within so many days of an operation to see if medical negligence was involved. It is a great protection for the family of the person who died and an equal protection for the doctor.

This old guy had undergone a very serious operation and had died subsequently from an unrelated cause. I was sent to observe the postmortem as part of my training; one of the more unpleasant parts of police work is dealing with dead bodies, and viewing a postmortem was the first step in getting a new constable used to it.

I'd never seen a dead body before, so stepping into the mortuary and being surrounded by dead bodies was unnerving. The place looked like something out of Frankenstein's laboratory, with body parts floating in preservation jars on shelves and the man laid out on a metal table under some bright lights. Two doctors, dressed in overalls, gloves, surgical masks and safety glasses, stood over the body. One of them motioned for me to watch over his shoulder during the initial incision.

He put a scalpel to the man's throat and slit the body from there to the top of the pubic bone. The body opened up as if the doctor had pulled on a zipper. It sounds macabre, but I was fascinated.

I started asking them questions about what I was seeing. After a few moments, one of the pathologists asked me if I'd like to take a closer look. He pointed me towards a shelf where the doctors kept their supplies and told me to suit up. I donned an overcoat, gloves, a surgical mask and safety glasses. The pathologist pointed out the various organs – the heart, the lungs, the kidneys and the liver. Something looked wrong with the man's liver. The brown organ was covered with tissue that looked damaged.

"Is that cancer?" I asked hesitantly.

"Once you get to be his age," the pathologist said, "you're bound to have something like that knocking around inside of you." But it wasn't the cancer that killed him; the cause of death was pneumonia, just as the doctors at the hospital had suspected.

As the procedure continued, I got involved in a hands-on fashion. The pathologist handed me the man's brain and pointed out a nearby scale; I weighed it and several other organs as well. I was hooked, amazed at the intricacies of the human body, the way all of the organs fit together and the architecture of the skeleton. The postmortem sounds morbid, but I found it beautiful. The Scriptures tell us we are "fearfully and wonderfully made," and when I saw inside a human body, I was struck with awe.

Because of my enthusiasm at the postmortem, my sergeant assigned me as a coroner's officer and sent me out whenever a sudden death occurred. It was a great time to minister to people, not in the sense of spreading the gospel but in coming alongside them during one of the worst moments of life. I would enter a house or a hospital room where somebody had died tragically and would be the first person there. My arrival was a starting point in the grieving process.

Often I had to ask very intimate things about the person who died as part of my investigation, and I couldn't come across as cold or callous. These questions often gave people who were overwhelmed with emotion something to focus on. For instance, if someone died at home, I had to ask details like, "What did the person eat for breakfast?" or "What was happening at the moment that they died?"

I loved conducting these interviews because I felt great job satisfaction in caring for people, especially compared to fighting with a drunk on a Saturday night, or catching a speeding driver, or writing up reports of stolen property or any of the other tasks that go along with being a police officer. I enjoyed dealing with the family of someone who had died, knowing that I had made life a bit easier for them.

My training as a minister was useful when something tragic happened and the sergeant needed someone who'd take a subtle or sensitive approach. A few times, people I'd dealt with rang up the police station afterwards to thank me. After a while, all of my shift sergeants knew that if there was a sudden death, they could send me. Most of them knew that I was a Christian and that I'd been studying for the priesthood before becoming a police officer. They used to call me "Graham from the God squad."

One night my sergeant called me and asked me to go with him to check on a scene where a young man was found dead in his car out on the moors. We found the small black sports car parked by the edge of a field. The driver, who was around twenty, had run a hose from the exhaust pipe to one of the windows of the car. He died from inhaling the exhaust fumes. The sergeant dropped me off and went back to pick up the undertaker.

A few minutes after my sergeant left, it started raining, slowly at first, then in a downpour. When the lightning started, I considered my alternatives. I could be miserable outside, getting soaking wet, or I could be dry and sheltered in the car. I got in.

It was bizarre to be in the middle of the moors with thunder crashing, lightning piercing the sky, and rain and hailstones beating down while sitting with someone who had just died. The young man was smartly dressed, wearing black trousers, a black jacket and a white shirt, and had stylishly cut blonde hair. He died with both hands gripping the steering wheel. I wondered what had gone so horribly wrong in his life that he thought suicide was his only option. I started to pray for him. That's one of the privileges of being a Christian – we can pray for the soul of the departed and for the family they have left behind. I knew there was nothing I could do for this boy, but I could ask God to look after him and to watch over his family.

After about forty minutes, my sergeant and the undertaker pulled up. I heard a call on my radio, "393, where are you?"

"I'm right here," I said.

My sergeant got out of the van and began looking around with his torch, wondering where I'd gotten off to. It was pitch black, and he couldn't see me. He walked right up to the car door and shined the torch in the window, jumping back in fright as I waved hello.

"You're sick," he said as he opened the door. "What are you doing in there?"

"Look," I said, "it's raining outside, so I went in the car to keep dry. I've been looking after this kid, praying for him."

"Doesn't it matter to you that he's dead?"

"No," I said, "it's not going to bother him that I'm sitting in here; he can't feel anything."

We loaded the body into a van and drove back into town. By the time we reached the mortuary, rigor mortis had set in. The young man's hands were stuck out in front of him as we laid him on the table. The sergeant had gone back to the police station, leaving me to assist the undertaker.

We had to undress the body, something I tried to do with as much dignity as possible. I always tried to treat a dead body with utmost respect because this was someone's loved one. The mortician and I tried to get the young man's shirt off gently. I grabbed hold of the young man's right arm and pushed it down by his side. We slipped the sleeve off, and just as I was about to reach over for the left arm, an icy hand shot up and grabbed hold of me.

I leapt up screaming, losing it completely. The hand literally had a death grip on my arm. When I was a kid, we used to see horror movies in which dead bodies started to move, but *The Night of the Living Dead* seems like *Winnie-the-Pooh* compared to the actual experience of a corpse taking hold of you.

Once I calmed down, the mortician was able to get my arm loose, and we finished undressing the body, me a little more warily this time. I started praying again, asking God to make sure the departed stayed still.

While my new job was going well, Kathy's pregnancy was not. The trouble started in early May. I had to spend a week away from home, and a friend of Kathy's had come from Scarborough to visit us. Kathy was experiencing all of the normal signs of early pregnancy, like nausea and morning sickness.

During the week I was away, Kathy developed a severe case of diarrhoea and was constantly rushing to the toilet. At first she thought it was another symptom of the pregnancy. When it didn't subside after a few days, she called her doctor, who assured her that it was normal and would soon go away. It didn't, and finally Kathy got so dehydrated that she was admitted to hospital. The doctors gave her intravenous fluids and several medications designed to relieve her symptoms, but none of them seemed to help.

Meanwhile, Kathy started worrying that she had colitis. Having worked in the gastroenterology department as a nurse in Scarborough, she thought her symptoms matched those of patients she'd seen. When I'd come and visit her, she complained that no one would listen to what she had to say about her condition. They put it down to being a result of the pregnancy and felt they'd soon have her sorted out. But every time I came to visit her, she looked thinner. She was very pale and losing weight fast.

Since I was on probation, I had to keep focused at work, trying not to let what was happening to Kathy distract me. That was difficult, as I now had two people to worry about, Kathy and the baby. I had just gotten used to the idea of becoming a father and now wondered how Kathy's illness would affect the baby.

The doctors finally diagnosed what Kathy had suspected earlier – she had colitis, a series of ulcers or sores that formed on her intestines. We were relieved that the diagnosis had finally been made but worried as things got worse as her pregnancy continued. As the baby grew, Kathy got sicker and lost more and more weight. When I would go into her private room, I would be hit by a wave of the smell of human waste, so overwhelming that I wanted to throw up. Kathy had been spending much of her time in the toilet and was literally shrinking before my eyes, turning into skin and bones as the weeks wore on. The only sign that she was pregnant was a little lump in her tummy, which wasn't really growing much at all. Her skin became baggy because she was losing weight so fast that it couldn't contract fast enough to keep up. The colitis also meant she was wracked with abdominal pain, which made even a simple activity like sleeping excruciatingly painful.

The best way to treat Kathy's condition was an operation to remove part of her colon, but the baby wouldn't survive the trauma of the procedure. Because the colitis could become life threatening, her doctors urged her to abort the baby. Their blunt advice was basically, "We think you should have an abortion. If you get rid of your baby, then we can operate on you and sort out your problem." But Kathy kept saying, "No, this is my baby. I can't do that."

We had tried unsuccessfully for five years to conceive, living through the heartbreaking monthly cycle of hoping that this would be the time that Kathy would be pregnant and then being disappointed over and over again. Trying to conceive for five years without success had eroded our dream of having children to love and nurture. We'd made plans to see a fertility consultant but didn't hold out much hope that we'd ever become parents.

While visiting some friends who are Pentecostal Christians, we shared our troubles, and they'd offered to pray for us. They put their arms around us and prayed that we would have a baby. It wasn't an overly emotional scene like something you would see on a television evangelist's programme; they just held us close and prayed. Later when we became pregnant, we believed this child was a gift from God, so we were going to hang on to the baby as long as we could. If the baby was going to die, then we could accept that. But we wouldn't choose abortion.

During the middle of this crisis, help often came from surprising places. My boss at the time was a police sergeant named Doreen. She was a big, strapping, old-fashioned police sergeant who could fight like the best of them. When there would be trouble at a pub and we'd have to break up a fight or arrest someone who was causing trouble, Doreen was the first one out of the car and into the fray. She used to give me a hard time. She nicknamed me "Ya-Ya," and if there was trouble, she'd yell at me, "Come on Ya-Ya, let's go get 'em!"

When Kathy was ill, Doreen was very supportive. One day I showed up for work, and she said, "Graham, today you're on foot patrol."

"All right," I said, "where's my beat?"

"Your beat is ward one at Friarage Hospital."

I must have had a puzzled look on my face, because that was Kathy's ward at the hospital. Doreen smiled at me. "Take your radio, and if we need you, we'll give you a call."

As often as she could, Doreen would station me at the hospital. If a sudden death occurred or an officer was needed at the hospital, Doreen would call me on the radio, and I'd go sort it out.

We'd stopped going to church when we moved to Northallerton. My placement at a church when I was in training had left a bad taste in my mouth. Most of the other ordinands were typically Anglican in background and thinking, and some believed their agenda was the most important thing in the world. Instead of the grace, forgiveness and love that I thought the church was supposed to be about, I witnessed a great deal of backbiting and politicking. So because I was working late nights and weekends, it was very easy to slip away from church and was actually a relief.

Even though we weren't attached to a church at the time, the local Anglican curate came and visited with Kathy. Some times he prayed with her, and other times he'd stay and keep her company while I was away. He also invited me around for tea to make sure I was all right. Some Catholic laypeople also came to Kathy's room to pray for her and encourage her. A web of people started to surround us, and it was as if God was reaching out and touching us through human hands. Alison, a friend of ours who is a charismatic Christian, came and prayed that God would heal Kathy. This kind of prayer, like the prayers that Kathy would get pregnant, was new to us. Kathy's obstetrician was also a Christian, and he prayed for her as well. He literally got down on his hands and knees by Kathy's bed and asked God to watch over Kathy and the baby.

All of these visitors would tell their friends about our situation, and soon a number of churches in Northallerton were praying for us. The Methodist church started to pray for us, so did a United Reformed church and a small nonconformist church as well.

Because I was on my own most of the time, people would bring meals over for me or invite me over for lunch or tea so I wouldn't be alone. It was the first time I'd seen this kind of practical expression of faith and love from groups of Christians. Though Kathy and I were going through a very difficult time, we knew we were not alone.

Meanwhile, my education as a police officer was continuing. New constables are constantly running into situations that aren't covered in the police training course, like what to do with a naked man who's been handcuffed to a lamppost.

I was on the high street at lunchtime on a Friday afternoon, having one of my two favourite meals in those days, a large order of fish and chips. (My other favourite was pizza, which accounted for the twenty pounds I'd put on since Kathy went into hospital.) I'd just taken a bite of fish when the dispatcher came over the radio.

"393, can you go to the marketplace and check on a naked man?"

This was certainly something new. I radioed in that I was on my way, anxious to see what was up.

The man was a lad in his twenties, handcuffed to the lamp-post and stark naked. Someone had painted rings around his eyes and a little black beard on his mouth and chin. As it was lunchtime, crowds of people in the marketplace were walking past him, laughing at his predicament.

"I'm really sorry about this," he said, as soon as I walked up. "I'm not doing this on purpose, honestly."

"Don't worry," I said, holding back a snicker. "So who did this?"

"They *were* my friends."

"Your friends?"

"I know," he said, sheepishly. "They're coming to my wedding tomorrow."

The culprits were his friends from work, who'd stripped off his clothes and handcuffed him to a lamppost right outside the office of the local newspaper as a prank.

As soon as the fire department showed up to cut this guy loose, so did a photographer from the newspaper. To save at least a scrap of his dignity, I took off my helmet and held it over his privates just before the photographer snapped a picture of the fireman cutting him free – a picture that appeared on the front page of the next day's paper.

Kathy stayed in hospital for most of the next six months of the pregnancy. Her doctors found some medication that stabilized her condition but were still pressing her to have an abortion so they could operate and provide a permanent solution. She felt trapped in the hospital and was desperate to get out, even if only for a night. She'd made friends with the nurses on the ward, and they conspired to help her leave, at least for a few hours. The doctors' orders were strict: if Kathy could keep enough food down that she'd gain three pounds, they'd let her go home for the night.

So the nurses would nick the telephone directory from the ward or all the spare magazines they could find – *Cosmopolitan* was a good option because it was heavy – and hide them under Kathy's dressing gown when they weighed her. Instantly, she miraculously gained a few extra pounds and could go home for the night. I would pick her up and take her home; when I would bring her back the next morning, those miracle pounds would have melted away.

Having a serious illness affected Kathy not only physically but emotionally, mentally and spiritually as well. Though Kathy hated being in the hospital, she also gained a sense of security from being there. Being outside the hospital made her feel vulnerable and fearful of any situation in which medical staff weren't around to help her. Something as simple as riding in the car at more than thirty miles an hour would give her a panic attack. Still, we cherished those few moments alone, to be able to talk and pretend for a moment that life was back to normal.

Sex, at least for the time Kathy remained in hospital, was out of the question. I was still in my twenties, and being celibate was not what I had in mind when we got married.

Apparently that thought had occurred to others as well. One day an acquaintance stopped by and asked me how I was holding up. We chatted for several minutes, and then he said, "You're wife's been in hospital for about six months now, hasn't she?"

"That's about right," I replied.

"So what have you been doing for sex?"

"I haven't been having any."

He put his arm around me and said, "Look, I can put that right. Come out with me tonight after work. I know a couple of girls who will do the business with you." The look on his face was sincere – he thought he was helping me out.

"Are you really suggesting that I have an affair?" I asked.

"You are never going to get caught, Graham," he said. "You just screw this girl, get it out of your system, and that's it."

"Thanks but no thanks," I replied.

Kathy would never have known if I had gone along. But I would have. As my friend talked to me about finding someone to "do the business with me," I tried to put myself in Kathy's position. What if I were the one who was helpless and vulnerable, barely able to get out of bed, and she came in and said, "Sorry, Graham, it's over, I'm finding someone new." At our wedding, Kathy and I promised to stay together, "for better for worse, for richer for poorer, in sickness and in health." We made a commitment, and I was going to stick by Kathy, even right unto death.

A few weeks later, in early November, a message came in over the radio that I was needed at the hospital. Kathy's condition had taken a turn for the worse. When I arrived, the consultant sat me down in the waiting area and told me the news. The strain of the colitis and the pregnancy was too much for Kathy, and her body was failing. "Your wife is dying, Mr Taylor. She's not going to make it through the night," the consultant said. "I'm sorry." He stayed for a few minutes and then left me alone in the waiting area.

My world crumbled. I was twenty-seven years old, and a doctor had just told me that my wife was going to die. Until that time, I'd been able to hold everything in – all the fear and worry about Kathy and the baby, the insecurity of feeling helpless to do anything about Kathy's being deathly ill. Stunned, I sat in the hard plastic chair, unable to think or move. The thought of going in and facing Kathy, knowing that she was going to die, was just too much. I wanted to pray, but the words wouldn't come out. So I went outside to clear my head with some fresh air.

As I stepped through the doors into the night, anger welled up inside me. I'd had a terrible temper for years, which had subsided since I became a Christian, but now it was back. I felt like I'd been sucker punched by this God who was supposed to love me, the God who spoke in London many years earlier that he'd find me a wife and a job. Suddenly my old, angry self was back with a vengeance, and instead of praying to God, I started swearing at him, using the old language that had been part of my life for so long.

"What are you doing this for? Why are you putting me through this? You've given me this woman, you've given me this baby, you do all these wonderful things for me. And now you're going to let her die. What kind of a God are you?"

I was furious with God. I thought, *Kathy's going to be all right, she's going to go to heaven. And I'll be stuck here on this planet without the one person I've ever really loved in my life.* I shook my fist at the skies. "You nasty, horrible, bald-headed old git – if only I could just stuff this fist right in your face, God!"

These were not exactly the prayers I learned in church. But I felt like a dam had burst inside, and all the anger and fear came pouring out. This swearing at God went on for some time and then subsided. Finally, when it was all out, I made my way back into hospital. Kathy needed me, and I wasn't doing her any good ranting and raving at God like a lunatic.

Doreen, my sergeant, was waiting in Kathy's room when I arrived. She was dressed in her civvies, or civilian cloths, sitting by Kathy's bed and watching her as she slept. "Sergeant, what are you doing here?" I asked, surprised to see her.

"Oh, I just thought I'd come and see her," Doreen said. That's the kind of person she was and what made her a great sergeant. She wasn't emotional or touchy-feely but was rock-steady and was always there when we needed her.

Once Doreen left, I sat down next to Kathy's bed, holding her hand as she drifted in and out of consciousness. She was in a great deal of pain and was very restless. I wanted to stay awake so she would know I was there. If she was going to die, I didn't want her to die alone. As the night wore on, I started praying again, not yelling at God but pleading with him to spare Kathy's life.

Sometime after midnight, I started to doze off. My head felt heavy and sleep started to creep over me. I struggled inside, with one part of my brain saying "Go to sleep," and another part saying "Stay awake." Several times I nodded off for a minute and then jolted back awake. Finally, I gave in. I thought, *I'll just put my head on the bed for two minutes, and I'll be fine.* At that point, I leaned over in my chair and was out.

While I was sleeping, Kathy was having a spiritual experience, as if God was right there in the room with her. A few nights earlier, she'd made a bargain with God, one that she described this way:

> I was too ill to sit up or read the Bible or do anything like that. All I could do was kind of pray in my head. At the time, I believed in God in a general way but didn't think about faith on a day-to-day basis. I thought, *If I live, I'm going to find out more about Jesus and God and be more committed.* So I said to God, "Look, if you get me out of this, I promise that I'll find out who you are instead of just plodding along and not really knowing anything about you."
>
> When Graham fell asleep beside me, I was too weak to move and was in a lot of pain from the pressure sores. It was excruciating, worse than the abdominal pain. I started crying out to God, saying, "Lord, please come and help me, just take this pain away. If I have to die to be free of the pain, I don't mind."
>
> At that point, dying would have been a relief.
>
> Then suddenly I felt as though my body had been lifted from the mattress. No one was there lifting me up, and I wasn't actually levitating or floating, but that's how it felt. A tremendous sense of relief and peace washed over me. I don't remember anything else because I slept the whole night through – probably the first time in months that I'd slept without waking up at least twenty times. When I

woke, it was morning, and when I saw the dawn that day, I knew I would live.

Kathy's condition seemed to stabilize after that night. We even managed one or two nights away with the help of the nurses and a few copies of *Cosmo*.

By late November, the baby was far enough along to be born safely. The doctors thought that Kathy could make it through the delivery but warned us that our baby, whom we knew was a girl, would likely be deformed because of the medicine that Kathy had to take. The drugs would likely lead to horrendous facial deformities, and the skin over our baby's face would literally be split in two. "I have to be honest with you, Mr Taylor," a consultant told us, "your daughter will come out looking like a monster."

Thank you very much, my daughter is going to be a monster, I thought to myself. In the days leading up to the birth, I started praying again. "Look God," I said over and over, "you have given me Kathy, you have given me this daughter, and you've gotten us through this terrible time. You can't have this baby be born a monster."

The doctors set a date of December first for the birth. They would induce labour by breaking Kathy's waters. They would get the baby out and then treat Kathy for her illness. A team was crowded around Kathy, and things went very fast once the consultant broke her waters.

I was terrified. I was sitting near Kathy's head, and I was so fearful that I buried my face in a pillow, unable to watch. All I could hear was the doctor's voice in my head, *"Mr Taylor, your daughter will be a monster. She'll be a monster. She'll be a monster."*

The nurses knew what was going on, and one of them touched me on the arm. "Mr Taylor," she said gently, "do you want to see your baby being born?"

"No," I responded. "I just can't bear it."

"Don't worry," she said. "It'll be fine."

I prayed over and over again, "Please God, please God – don't let her be a monster. Don't let her be a monster."

Kathy gave a loud yell, and I heard the cry of my daughter for the first time. The doctor held her in his arms, and I caught of glimpse of Hannah from the side. I started to panic because she seemed blue. Was she dead? I wanted to shout at the doctors to do something, but they had already swept into action. One of them wiped Hannah down while another placed her under a warming light and held an oxygen mask over her. She started to breathe and then to scream. She was alive.

The nurse walked over to her and said, loud enough for me to hear, "Oh, what a lovely baby girl."

"Let me see," I said. I stood over her and saw that she was beautiful. At the end of her nose was a tiny mark, the size of a thumbnail print, where some of the skin had split and then closed together. It was as if God had said, "And you thought she'd be born a monster. Look at her, she's beautiful." It was a moment of pure joy.

The next months were full of challenges because Kathy got worse before she got better. After giving birth, the hormones in her body changed, which caused complications, including kidney trouble. She had an operation for her colitis and faced a long recovery. She would, all told, spend eighteen months in and out of hospital. Since she stayed in hospital for an extended period, I was on my own as a new parent. When I was working night shifts, Hannah stayed at home with me during the day, and then I'd take her back to the hospital at night, and the nurses would look after her on the children's ward. Both of our families lived fifty miles away in Scarborough, so there was no practical way for them to look after Hannah.

Even after Kathy was released from hospital, she was still weak and faced a long recovery. She and Hannah went and lived with her mother in Scarborough for a few months. Kathy was not strong enough to be on her own, and I had to be at work most of the time. I would come down to Scarborough on my days off.

During this stressful time, the best advice came from Police Constable Barningham, one of the older constables on the force. If he saw me getting stressed out on the job, he'd stop me and say, "Graham, will it really matter in twenty years' time? Will anyone remember it twenty years from now?"

If I said no, which was usually the case, he'd say, "Then don't worry about it."

That put life into perspective. Not a lot of things are really worth losing sleep over. Kathy's health was. But even then, worrying was not helping me. It didn't help me care for Kathy better or do my job better. It just worked me up and made it harder to get anything done. I eventually realised that I had to stop worrying and let God sort it out.

I had to learn to relax and float instead of swim. The trouble with us humans is that we think we are in charge when we are not. We have to realise that a greater power is in charge of our lives. That's not predestination; it's just that no matter what you do in life, God will always have the greater say.

Kathy's illness taught me that people are very resilient, much more than we realise. We tap into that resiliency by relaxing into our situation, accepting our circumstances and then getting on with the job at hand. I had to accept that Kathy was ill, that nothing I could do would change that and that she could still die. I just had to make the best of the situation.

When Kathy and Hannah left the hospital, we bought an enormous pram and took her with us wherever we went. This was before car seats, so when we'd have to drive, I'd stick the pram in the back of the car and wedge it between the back-seats – which, looking back, was a highly dangerous thing to do. But we didn't know any better at the time.

We really enjoyed being new parents. The best times were the simple outings, like going to the North Yorkshire Moors and sitting on a picnic rug while watching Hannah crawl round, or when we were in Scarborough, taking her out on the beach and watching her eat sand. The most pleasurable thing was seeing Hannah grow and knowing that God had brought us through this horrendous part of life, and now we had this wonderful little girl.

And when Kathy was well enough, we started going to church again. The United Reformed church held a service every Wednesday at lunchtime, and we'd go and have communion. Hannah would cry or sleep or, when she was older, crawl around on the floor. But no one seemed to mind. We fell into a community of people who believed in God and who were committed to and loved each other.

So many Christians never go near a church because they have been hurt by people like I was. Someone talked about us behind our backs, or the minister said something that we don't agree with, so we disappear from church, trying to maintain some sort of faith in Jesus on our own. When we do that, we miss the best part of faith, which is coming together as believers and loving and caring for each other.

In the long run, God used Kathy's illness to draw me back into church. Which is quite sneaky, if you ask me.

8

OFF THE ROOF

At the end of my probationary period in 1989, I was assigned to a rural beat in Swainby, a village on the edge of the North Yorkshire Moors. I was almost always on my own, with no backup, so I constantly improvised. Sometimes it worked, like the night I caught the poachers.

I was miles from the nearest town, driving down a lonely road near a fish farm when I came across a car with five guys sitting in it. It was after midnight, and something just didn't feel right. By that time of night, the roads were always deserted. A check on the car's tag revealed the owner's address was about forty miles away. *So what are these people doing way out here in the middle of the night, forty miles from home?* A routine traffic check was in order. Turning my car around, I pulled up right behind them and parked.

"Hi guys," I said, walking up to the car, a smile on my face. In cases like this, it's best to play the friendly, thick officer. Acting dumb disarms people and makes them feel as if they have the upper hand.

The driver rolled down the window, and out poured the telltale smell of fish. Still, I acted like nothing was unusual.

After chatting with them for a few minutes, I asked the driver, "Can I just check your boot to see if your spare tyre is okay?"

By reflex, the driver opened his boot, and sure enough, a load of wriggling fish stared up at me. They were trout, straight from the fish farm.

"Oh dear," I said. "Are these flying fish and have they just flown into your boot?"

A few choice curses started flying in the back of the car. Before they could think of a plan, I pulled the driver out of the car, away from the other guys, and had a talk with him.

"Look," I said, "this is your car, right?"

"Yeah," he said.

"Your name is on the tag?"

"Yeah."

I said, "I've radioed your car in and I've radioed your name in. So whatever happens out here is up to you. I know there are five of you and one of me. But we all know who you are. So don't play the fool."

"Yeah, all right."

Clearly a man of few words.

We walked back to the others, and I laid out their options. They were all under arrest, but there was no way the five of them could fit in my car. I could call in a van, which would take an hour to get here, load them up and leave their car behind. They'd have a thirty-mile walk back in the morning when they got out.

"Or," I said, "we could be sensible about this. You can drive yourselves to the police station, we can put your car in the car park, and when you are released, you can drive away."

They decided to be sensible, and we got to the station without incident. Sadly, the shift sergeant didn't seem to share my ingenuity. When I told him how I'd got them there, he looked at me despairingly.

This sort of thing happened all the time. I remember a stormy night when a group of five guys in their twenties took off in a car on the moors. When they saw me chasing them, they pulled over by the side and scattered into the forest of oak, birch and hazel trees surrounding the road.

So there were me and these kids. They'd have to come back to the car at some point – they were too far out on the moor to walk back easily – so I could either wait them out or go in after them. But going into the woods really wasn't an option; the trees were so thick that I could walk right past them and never see them, and they could easily wait for me to go by and jump me from behind. I radioed the sergeant and explained my situation and asked him to send a dog officer out. I might not be able to find them in the woods, but it'd be no trouble for the dog.

Then a thought occurred to me. I stuck my head inside the car and started making dog noises, howling and barking and banging my hand against the roof of the car. When a dog's in a police car, there's always a banging noise.

"It's the police!" I yelled at the woods. "I've got a dog! If you don't come out by the time I count to five, I'm going to send the dog in." I ducked back in the car, made some more dog noises, then popped my head out and started counting.

"One, two, three …"

"Don't do it, it's all right, it's all right!" A kid dressed in jeans and a T-shirt walked out with his hands in the air. "I give up! I give up!"

"On the ground," I yelled. "Get on your face with your hands out in front of you."

Once he was down on the ground, I raced over and slapped the cuffs on him and pulled him up to his feet, dragging him to the car as quickly as I could. A few feet from the car, he realised he'd been had.

"It's a police car!" he said.

"Yeah, it's a police car. What of it?"

"But where's your dog?" In our area, dog officers always drive vans. That thought hadn't occurred to him before he'd given himself up.

I smiled at him. "Woof, woof."

"You can't – " he started.

"I already have," I said and pulled him towards the car door. As I was ducking his head in, he called out, "It's a trick! He hasn't got a dog."

About five minutes later, the dog van arrived, and out stepped Constable Brewster. Constable Brewster was a typical old copper – a no-nonsense, fantastic policeman. We talked for a minute, and I pointed out where these guys had gone into the woods.

"Right, lads," he said. "It's the police. If you don't come out in five, I'm going to send the doggie."

He paused a second, then started the count: "One, two, three, four, five."

No sign of movement in the trees. So the constable opened the back door of the van, and out came his Alsatian police dog.

"Right," he said. "Go get him."

The dog bounded into the woods. About a minute later, we heard, "Ahh! Ahh! Get him off me. It's a dog!"

We followed the cries till we found a kid with the dog's teeth clamped around his arm. He'd tried to fight the dog, and the dog thought he was playing and grabbed hold and wouldn't let go. We marched the kid out of the woods, and soon afterwards the rest of the lads followed. Mission accomplished.

But my improvisations didn't always have such good outcomes.

One day I received a call that some burglars were breaking into a chemist's shop in a village. When I arrived, the next-door neighbour said, "Yeah, they were up on the roof, but they're gone now."

I hate heights. I can't stand them at all. But someone had to go see if the burglars had done any damage, and I was the only officer around. After taking a deep breath, up I went. I'd reached the roof ridge and was just thinking, *I hope nobody's up there*, when I saw the guys illuminated in my torchlight. The building had what they call a double eave – two pitched roofs on the outside, with a flat bit of roof in between. Three burglars were standing on the flat bit.

Once they saw me, they panicked and rushed at me, hoping, I suppose, to knock me off the roof. It was a long way down, about thirty feet.

It's either them or me, I thought. I pulled out my truncheon and ran at them, screaming like a psychopathic banshee. The sight of a seventeen-stone fat guy with red hair waving a truncheon stopped two of the burglars, who turned and ran the other way. The other guy didn't. He kept coming at me.

We started fighting, him with his fists, me with my truncheon. I dropped my torch on the roof, so that I'd have a free hand to grab hold of him if I could. After a minute or two, he'd had enough and decided to jump. The thing was, I had just gotten my hand wedged firmly down the collar of his jacket. So as he flung himself off the roof, I knew I would be going down with him. I didn't have time to be terrified about falling, because one minute we were on the roof and the next minute we were off.

As I landed, I thought, *Thank God for good gardeners*. The homeowner next door had just dug out all of his flowerbeds and refilled them with manure and heaps of new soil. So we had a relatively soft landing.

When I picked the would-be burglar up, he was covered in dirt, manure and blood. Since we were both a bit battered and bruised, I drove him to the hospital in Malton, about thirty miles away. It was the quickest thing to do; it'd take twice as long to go by ambulance, which would have to come from York, forty miles away, or from Scarborough. It was a lot easier just to hop in the car and go.

The incident on the roof was typical for me. I was always the first guy through the door, always ready to take someone on, never worried about what would happen. I had been like that for years. Most of my adventures ended like that night on the roof – a few bumps and bruises, an occasional trip to the hospital, but everything turning out all right in the end.

In October of 1989, I had a horrendous feeling that my mum and dad were going to die. They weren't sick; both of them were very fit for their age (Mum was in her midseventies and Dad in his mideighties). But I couldn't get the thought out of my head that they wouldn't be around long, and I just wanted to be near them. When Christmas came and went and I was still thinking this way, I asked my superintendent for a move.

There were no vacancies in Scarborough at the time. The nearest vacancies were in Kirkbymoorside and Pickering. Kathy and I took a Saturday to go and have a look at both towns to see what we thought. Pickering was the closest to Scarborough, and there we found a lovely little semi-detached house at 12 Ruffa Lane. We came back and told my superintendent that I would take the vacancy in Pickering.

We arrived in March of 1990, and my Dad died in May. He was eighty-five and suffered a stroke in April and never recovered. On the first of May, I went to see him at the hospital; he was very poorly. He couldn't speak, and though he was fighting hard to hang on, it was clear that he didn't have long to live.

On 2 May, I drove to Northallerton for a computer-training course in the morning. On the way back, I got a radio message. I had borrowed a police car for the drive, and the car's call sign was "Foxtrot Pappa 3-5." The message came in, "Foxtrot Pappa 3-5, can you ring this office? We have a message for you."

"Is it my Dad?" I asked.

"Yes, can you ring in?"

This was long before mobile phones had come to North Yorkshire, so I pulled over at a friend's house in the village and used his phone. When I reached my sergeant, he said that my dad had died and that I should come straight back to the station instead of finishing my shift.

Later that day, I sat in our garden and thought about my dad, the tears streaming down my face. Our garden had a view of St Peter and St Paul's church in Pickering with its tall spire. The burning, orange-red sun was setting behind the church, and the spire was surrounded by wonderful sunlight. As I gazed up, I cried for my father and for all the pain I'd caused him. We'd long since made up, and he told me that what I'd done as a kid "didn't matter," but I regretted it still.

As I sat there, Hannah came up to me and put a rock in my lap. She said softly, "A rock for you, Daddy," and toddled off. "A rock for you, Daddy." Staring at the cross in the sunset, I felt like God was speaking directly to me – that despite being completely broken over losing my earthly father, I had God, my heavenly father, to rely on. The sun set further and further behind the church, and the image of the church became clearer and clearer. In my mind, I had a picture of my Dad's life going down and fading away, yet the presence of God remaining with me.

On the day my father died, my mother was diagnosed with breast cancer. It was an aggressive cancer, and it had spread into her bones. She went through all the treatments, had surgery and radiation therapy, but she was not long for this world. She was seventy-two, and my father's death had taken from her the will to live. If he was gone, what was the point of her going on?

My mother's decline was slower than my father's, and we had time to say goodbye from May, when she was diagnosed, till August, when she died. One afternoon, as we sat on the sofa in the front room of the house on Maple Drive, I began apologizing for all that I'd done as a teenager, for treating her so badly. Neither of my parents had ever said as much as a word about it since I'd come home from London years earlier.

"Graham," she said, "I love you. This is what being a mother is all about. It doesn't matter. I love my children, no matter what. I love you."

Those were the words I desperately needed to hear. I wanted to know that despite what I had done to her – despite the hurt and the heartache and the pain and the misery I had caused her – my mother still loved me.

On the day my mother died, I held her hand and prayed with her. She was at peace and ready to die. In the months beforehand, I'd been praying frantically that she'd be healed. I begged God to make her well. And nothing happened. Then one night as I was praying for her, I felt as if God answered my pleas with a question. "How long do you want her to live?" My mum was seventy-two and ready to die, but I wasn't ready to let her go. Many of us have this trouble – we place too much emphasis on this life. But as a Christian, I believe this life isn't everything, and there comes a point when we've got to let the illness "be unto death."

Part of my maturing as a Christian and, much later, my experience as a priest, was learning about the reality of death. Not always running around saying, "Let's get this person healed." But getting the theology of death into my head. There is a time to die, and it might not be in three score years and ten. God doesn't judge quantity; he judges quality, and he can pack an awful lot into a very short life.

Did my parents know God? That's something I wondered about after they were gone. My mum let me pray with her, but she didn't profess to be a Christian in the way that Kathy and I do. But I think that, in their own way, both my parents knew God.

The Bible is very clear that Jesus asks us for faith the size of a mustard seed; that's all we need. But what about people who have never heard of Jesus? Are they condemned to hell and cut off from God? I believe that in order to go to heaven, we have to accept Jesus as our Saviour. And some people will go to hell out of their own willingness to go there. But I also believe that others will be in heaven by virtue of a very simple faith, one the size of a mustard seed. During my time as a priest, I often saw small, quiet signs of a person's faith, mostly unseen by the outside world.

We only become Christians when we accept Christ. And many people in this world have done that in their own simple way. They may not go to church, they may not profess their faith in the language that I would want them to, but they still know Jesus. If we have faith the size of a mustard seed and ask Jesus to save us, he will. He certainly saved me over and over again.

After my parents died, I decided to return to the Church of England ordination scheme. Even though I had settled into my career as a police constable, somewhere in the back of my mind, I heard the echo of the voice that had called me into ministry. It was a voice I knew I couldn't ignore forever. I felt an obligation to go through with the training, so I worked out what I thought was a compromise with God: I would go back and complete my training and then continue working as a police officer.

I wasn't too sure about priesthood as a profession – that is, going off to theological college for training and then getting sent to a parish, where I would be the full-time minister for the village. I wanted to explore a new way of doing ministry – by being both a priest and a police officer.

Before going back to the director of ordinands, I enrolled at St Andrew's Bible College. At that time, it was out of fashion to believe in Jesus in a traditional way. I knew that I would encounter intelligent, well-read liberal theologians at theological college who would find it satisfying to pull my faith apart. I wanted to be able to engage them on matters of faith in an intelligent, not a reactionary, manner. So I spent three years at St Andrews. There I got a solid grounding in theology and in New Testament Greek and other biblical studies. When I finished at St Andrews, I felt ready to return to my ministerial training.

When I finally arrived in the Church of England theological college, one of my tutors began his first lecture by saying that "Jesus gets in the way of Christianity." Another told me to "put my Bible away and use my brain for a change."

I soon discovered that liberals – at least the ones I met in theological college – weren't liberal after all, if the word means being open to other ideas or points of view. If students agreed with their liberal theology, everything was fine. But my tutors became very illiberal as soon as I started disagreeing with them. For example, if one of our tutors pronounced that God was now a "she," we were expected to go along. If someone – usually me – raised an objection based on the Bible, the response was swift and cruel. Typical comments were, "That's your ignorance showing" or "That's caveman mentality."

In response, I caused as much trouble as I could, going out on a limb to wind up my tutors. If a tutor was bothered by evangelicals, I'd pretend to be a rabid evangelical. Or if a tutor didn't believe in miracles, I'd go out of my way to bring up the topic in discussion. One tutor hated the apostle Paul, so in the middle of lectures, I would bring him up, watching as my tutor got infuriated and lost his temper and composure. It was wicked of me – Paul himself tells us to avoid these kinds of arguments – but I couldn't resist the temptation to create a stir.

For the practical part of my training, I was assigned as an assistant curate of the church of St Peter and St Paul in the village of Pickering. During the weeks, I remained a police officer; during the weekends, I served at the church, under the supervision of the vicar. The arrangement sometimes brought a certain amount of excitement. Just after I was ordained, one of my supervisors called me into the police station in Malton. "I'm not going to have a f---ing vicar lording it over the other constables. When you're on duty, you're PC Taylor, plain and simple." I later learned that this particular supervisor had been at a party with my bishop, and they had been arguing over whose side I belonged to. My bishop had said, "You've got one of my boys there on the police force." My supervisor had replied, "No, you've got one of my boys in the church."

The only serious conflict came one Sunday when I was hearing someone's confession and they told me about a crime they had committed – they had stolen something valuable and felt tremendous guilt over it. Two days later, I went to the police station and overheard two constables discussing the crime. I couldn't divulge the name of the perpetrator because of the seal of the confessional. And as it was a property matter and no one's life was at risk, I could keep the secret in good conscience. But I told the person who confessed that they had to make amends for their crime. So they gave themselves up to the police, and the dilemma was solved.

For the most part, the two jobs fit together seamlessly. I could continue to minister to people but not have to deal with the hierarchy of the church.

Kathy looked out the window at three o'clock in the morning and wondered what her husband had got himself into this time. A police car, siren wailing, was in hot pursuit of a black

Mitsubishi Shogun four-wheel drive that screeched past our house on Ruffa Lane. I was plastered to the side window of the Shogun.

Five minutes earlier, I had been inside the police car on traffic patrol when we stopped the Shogun on suspicion of drunk-driving. The driver rolled down the window as I stepped up to the truck. I leaned over and peered into the driver's face. He reeked of alcohol.

"Please step out of the car," I said.

"What's the trouble, constable?" the driver said.

"Please step out of the car."

He didn't budge.

"Please step out of the car."

This went on for another minute. No matter what I said, the driver refused to move.

Fearing that he'd try to drive off, I leaned through the window to snatch the keys from the ignition. As my hand closed on the keys, he rolled up the window, trapping my arm and shoulder. When I let go of the keys, he started the car and drove away, with me hanging on for dear life. I didn't dare grab the driver for fear of causing a crash.

Thankfully, I was with a partner that night, so the other officer gave chase. The Shogun rounded the corner onto Ruffa Lane, and somewhere along the road, the driver realised that I was attached to the car. He was so drunk that I don't think it registered before then. He pressed the button, the window dropped down and I fell off the Shogun. My partner stopped the police car, and I jumped back in to continue the chase. As we were in a Vauxhall Carlton police car, which is designed for high speeds, and he was in a four-wheel drive, it was only a matter of time before we caught up with him.

Something entertaining was always happening in Pickering. As rural police, we were Mr Fix-It, and whenever people got in a mess, they'd ring us. Cat's up a tree? Ring the police to get him down. Husband tried to mend the washing machine and got his head stuck inside? Don't worry; the police will sort him out. As policemen, we just got on with the job. Even if it was chasing down a kangaroo on the loose.

The manager of a local hotel rang just after teatime with trouble. The hotel kept wild animals to entertain guests, and someone had decided that putting a kangaroo on display would draw more business. They built a four-foot-high fence around the kangaroo's enclosure, but the kangaroo had jumped right over it.

"It's a wild kangaroo, and it's on the loose," the manager said. "Can you come and get it?"

I'd never seen a kangaroo before, but I'd seen a wallaby at a zoo. On my drive over, visions of something about two feet tall – the size of a cute little wallaby – ran through my head. How much trouble could a kangaroo be? In case you're wondering, an adult kangaroo can be more than four feet tall and weigh close to two hundred pounds. That's a big animal.

When I arrived, the kangaroo was nibbling grass on the grounds of the hotel, just outside the tennis courts. "You could try to get him in there," the manager suggested, pointing to the courts, since the small fenced enclosure was no good.

Pulling out my truncheon, I walked very slowly towards the kangaroo, which paid me no heed. As I crept nearer to it, it hopped away. Little by little, I herded him towards the tennis courts. When we were nearly there, I raised my truncheon to shoo it into the tennis courts. Instead of going in, the animal jumped at me. I dove out of the way as it sailed by, its tail nearly hitting me in the head.

Time to call in the troops.

"3-9-3 to any units in the area," I called over the radio. "I've got a wild kangaroo, and it's just attempted to assault a police officer. If anyone would like to come and assist, you're welcome."

Everybody turned up. "Where's this kangaroo then?" my sergeant said after he pulled up. For the next hour, we chased it back and forth around the hotel grounds. It was like a scene out of Monty Python. There's ten coppers with truncheons drawn, helmets on, riot shields in hand, and here's the kangaroo, bounding away the second we get near it.

At the end of the hour, we gave up. All ten of us collapsed on the ground, absolutely knackered. "What do we do now?" I asked my sergeant.

"Would you look at that," one of the constables remarked. We turned and watched the kangaroo hop into the tennis courts of its own accord. Before it could change its mind, we shut the gate behind it.

"Right, your problem now," I called to the hotel manager as we left. "Whatever you do, don't open that gate.

The kangaroo incident wasn't the oddest occurrence of my police career. That came on the night I was working with Traffic Constable Dave Gowdy. It was in the middle of winter, well below freezing. In the early hours of the morning, someone knocked timidly on the back door of the police station. When Dave answered it, he found a young guy standing there, shivering and turning blue with cold.

"What's the matter?" Dave asked.

"I've had a terrible, terrible accident," the man said. "You've got to help me. I jumped over the hedge for a wee and pulled my zip up too quickly. And now I'm stuck." He'd driven his motorcycle six miles in the freezing cold in a very uncomfortable, half-naked condition.

The police training course doesn't include a section on how to help motorcyclists in this kind of state. But we eventually freed him from his predicament. Needless to say, he was very grateful.

Police officers see it all. Sometimes – as with the mad kangaroo or our motorcyclist in trouble – they can sort things out with no harm done. Other times things happen that are so horrible that not even the best police officers can set them right. All they can do is pick up the broken pieces that are left behind.

9

"Where's Your God Now?"

The car, carrying three people, had been hit by a lorry near Kirkbymoorside and was thrown into a gulley by the side of the road. My sergeant, Vince, and I had to go down and carry the bodies out, for they were too mangled for the fire brigade or ambulance crew to even touch.

We stood by the wreck, wondering how on earth we could get the bodies out. When I got down on my knees to take a closer look, Vince asked, "Are you going to pray now?" At first I thought he was trying a bit of gallows humour to get our minds off the gruesome task, but his face was serious.

"Okay," I said. "Lord God, please be with us in this; we really do need your help here."

"Right," Vince said. "Come on, let's get them out."

Vince pried the door open and began cutting the seat belt that held one of the victims in place. The man was in a dreadful state, covered in blood with seemingly every bone in his body broken. Standing in the mud at the bottom of the bank, we handled him as gently as possible, easing his floppy corpse into a body bag. Covered in mud, we slipped and crawled our way up the hill while carrying him.

On that bank near Kirkbymoorside, I realised I was numb inside. Here was a human tragedy – three people killed in a horrific accident – but after eight years of dealing with death, I felt nothing for them. Vince and I had a job to do, and that was all. We did it with kindness and respect, but I was completely desensitised.

All told, I attended to about eighty deaths in my years on the police force. Sometimes we'd go for a month or two without one, and then they'd come in waves. The summer in particular seemed a popular time to die.

I'll never forget Harold, who died on 8 August. We figured the date out because he bought a newspaper every day, and the last one we found bore that date. Harold lived alone, and at first no one noticed that he was gone. A week went by, and then another, and finally almost two months had passed when a neighbour called the police station to report Harold missing.

The beat officer who went to the house reported an awful stench. The inspector asked Vince and me to identify the body. There wasn't much left of him, the inspector told us, just his bones and his hair, still in his distinctive hairstyle.

We entered the house teeming with flies and maggots on 29 September, dressed in full bodysuits and masks. Harold was lying on his bed when he died, and his body had rotted so badly that it had melted into the mattress. He'd been there long enough for two cycles of flies to live and breed on him. All that was left to identify him was his hair, lying on the pillow.

Despite my mask, the stench filled my nose and mouth. I couldn't get the taste out of my mouth for a week. The image of Harold lying there is burned into my memory and will never fade away.

Being a police officer means carrying these horrendous experiences for years. The kind of horrific scenes that most people may see once in a lifetime, police see daily. No wonder so many constables burn out or have breakdowns. For years, they pick up the bits and pieces of people's broken lives till finally one day their brain says, "I have had enough of this – it's too much to take."

For me, the burnout process started on the day I had two sudden deaths in one eight-hour shift. First was a call in the morning about a woman who had died in bed. The second was about a middle-aged man who'd hung himself. After cutting him down and hauling him to the morgue, I stopped by a minor accident on the road leading to Pickering.

When I arrived on the scene, one of the drivers was cursing out the other for putting a scratch in his car. I stepped in between them, trying to get the irate driver to calm down.

"He scratched my car," he kept saying with great indignation. "He's going to pay for this."

At first glance, neither car seemed damaged at all. "I don't see any damage," I said. "What this you're on about?"

He walked to the back of his car and pointed to a small scratch on the back bumper. "It's four inches long, I've measured it," he said. He was so livid that his face had turned bright red.

"I'll pay for the damage," the other driver said.

"That's right, you will," started the irate driver. He had a nice car, a Bentley, but the damage was miniscule.

"Right," I said. "Are either of you dying?"

"No."

"Are there any injuries?"

"No."

Looking straight into the eyes of the Bentley driver, I said, "I've just come from a sudden death where a man hanged himself, and his family are distraught. Do you think this accident compares with that?"

They both went completely quiet. I told them to go away, swap each other's registration numbers and sort it out. This was not a police matter.

"You can't leave," said the Bentley driver. "I have rights."

"If you think this is a problem, then you don't have a life," I said, turning on my heel and walking back to my police car.

"What's your number?" he demanded.

"It's 393," I said. "What are you going to do about it?"

"I am going to file a complaint."

"Okay," I said, "the station is just up the road. Turn left, go down to the end of the street, and it's on the corner."

This is crazy, I thought.

The same thought occurred to me a few weeks later when I was at a retreat run by my theological college in Durham. The weekend's programme consisted not of prayer but of "trust-building exercises." About sixteen of us were in the class, and for one exercise, we were divided into pairs. One person was blindfolded and had to walk along a path, being led by the other.

Afterwards our tutor led us to a field where a picnic dinner had been set up. Food and wine were on the table, but before we started eating, we were instructed to take off our shoes and socks, gather in a circle and hold hands. The grass was wet and cold, but apparently that was part of the exercise.

"I want you to close your eyes and feel the earth vibrate through your body," our tutor called out. "As the vibrations move through your body, I want you to hum along with them." The class sounded like a bunch of pregnant cows, standing out in a field and mooing. Once the humming started, I dropped out and sat on nearby rock, watching the rest of the class.

I felt like I was in a madhouse and couldn't for the life of me imagine what "feeling the earth's vibrations" had to do with the Christian faith or the Church of England. A few years earlier, I might have gone along for fear of being embarrassed. But being on the police force had toughened me up, and I didn't worry what anyone else thought. I had also come to terms with what was going on in the Church of England, realising that I didn't have to change my beliefs to get along. I was finally secure in what I believed and who I was.

I went into the police force and thought I had escaped God's call. In response, God used my experiences as a copper to prepare me for ministry. I'd need a strong back and broad shoulders to be a vicar, because ministry is a hard business.

There were some bright spots in our life in Pickering. One of the brightest was the birth of Abigail, our second daughter, in 1991. When Kathy first told me she was pregnant, I began to panic. As much as I loved Hannah, the thought of Kathy going through another pregnancy was terrifying. After all, this time I might lose her. And the thought of going through another eighteen months of her going in and out of hospital was more than I could bear.

But things were different this time. Kathy became ill but only mildly so. She spent a month in hospital late in the pregnancy – a difficult time but one that we managed to survive. Abigail was perfect, as beautiful as her sister. And for a time, we were very happy in Pickering.

In the fall of 1992, several of us were called to a house in Pickering where a little girl had died. Flossie was seven years old and had been playing out in the garden when suddenly she fell over dead. One minute she was full of life, the next she was gone.

Flossie's mother was understandably devastated. After we had been there a while, one of the other officers took the mother inside to help her calm down. It would be some time before the coroner's ambulance would come and take the little girl's body away. Since we didn't know how Flossie had died, the coroners would want to photograph the scene. It didn't seem right to just put a cover on the body and leave her there.

Before she went inside, Flossie's mother begged me to stay with her daughter. It was getting late, and she couldn't bear the thought of her little girl lying there all alone in the dark.

"Please, don't leave her," she begged, as one of the other constables led her away.

I promised to stay, so I sat in the garden and held Flossie's hand. She was a little blonde-haired girl, dressed in a riding suit. I'll never forget her because she looked so much like my daughter Hannah, who was about the same age.

All I could do during the two-hour wait was hold Flossie's hand and pray. Some of the time I asked God, "Why? Why did this have to happen to this little girl?" but there were no answers. (Later on, we found out that she died of natural causes. It was just one of those tragic deaths that happen sometimes.) Most of the time, however, I just asked God to be there and to take care of her family.

When I got home, the first thing I did was go into Hannah's room. She was sleeping peacefully, with the same hair, the same little pretty face as Flossie. I sat down, held her hand and wept. Of course, Hannah's hand was warm. She was alive and was going to wake up in the morning. Little Flossie wasn't.

The next day, I had to go back to the house. As I finished up and was getting ready to go, Flossie's mother stopped me, asking, "Are you a Christian?"

"I am, actually," I replied, not sure why she was asking.

"Yeah, we thought you were," she said. "I could just sense that feeling of love from you. Thank you."

I never really knew when God was using me in situations, but looking back, I can see his hand gently guiding me. Sometimes I feel very far away from God – mostly of my own making – but he's always there, and no matter how far I fall, he lifts me up.

Even though I knew God had used me that night in the garden, something started to crack inside. I'd seen too much death, too much tragedy, too much violence.

In 1993, the drug ecstasy had just begun to permeate our area of Yorkshire. I had started doing some undercover work – hiding out in buildings, taking photographs of dealers, that sort of thing. Violent crime was up, with a lot of people getting spaced out on drugs and alcohol. They called it the "summer of love."

Around ten o'clock one Friday night in June, I was on patrol in Pickering when I got a call that someone had busted a shop window in the town's marketplace. It was nothing out of the ordinary, probably the work of some kid who'd had too much to drink.

Pickering was a main market town for the area, and kids from the surrounding villages would come in for a few pints and some fish and chips from the takeaway. Kids can be drinking and be fairly sober in a pub, but when they walk out into the fresh air, something seems to happen. We never had any trouble inside the pubs, but outside was another story. We were usually on patrol at night, keeping an eye on potential trouble spots.

I got to the shop, and a witness identified the guy who'd broken the window. He was still hanging around on the high street; a young guy of about twenty who was a good kid for the most part. I knew him from the streets.

I found him standing outside the Black Swan, an old, brick pub towards the end of the high street. I arrested him, saying, "Look, come back to the station with me. I'll interview you and have you back by closing time." My plan was to put him before the sergeant, do a quick interview and have him bailed. That way, he could come back in the morning, after I'd gotten a statement from the shopkeeper and from some of the witnesses.

It was fairer than keeping him in jail overnight. He would be in and out within thirty-five minutes.

This kind of arrest was a regular event. I'd done it hundreds of times, so I wasn't expecting any trouble. There was no need even to handcuff him. He agreed to come along quietly and climbed into the back of the police car.

It was a warm, clear summer's evening, a pleasant night to be out on the town. But all of that was about to change. Unbeknownst to me, while I was putting this kid in the car, a group of his mates had swarmed out of the Black Swan pub. They saw their friend in trouble and decided to come to his rescue.

I was making my way round to the front of the car when pandemonium exploded around me. One minute I was all alone, the next I was surrounded by an angry mob. They pushed me up against the car and began punching and kicking me while swearing at the top of their lungs. Fortunately I had my radio switched on, which I usually forgot to do, and I put out the emergency call "10-9," or "officer in distress." Since I was the only officer on patrol, I had no idea how long it would take for backup to arrive.

That night, I was nothing like Clint Eastwood playing *Dirty Harry*; I was simply not cool. Later I heard the tape of my call for help. It was just "10-9, Pickering marketplace, I am being attacked, I am being attacked" and then shouting and screaming. In the background were the thuds and thumps of me getting hit and hitting back and the sound of me being pushed against the police car. It was utter bedlam.

I had my truncheon with me, but it was stuck in my pocket and I couldn't get it out. I didn't dare turn my attention away from the mob. There were twenty-five or thirty of them, all around eighteen to twenty years old. They were mostly boys who were farmers or bricklayers, dressed in jeans and T-shirts, but a few girls were also in the mob.

One who hit me the hardest was a girl. I remember seeing her out of the corner of my eye and thinking, *She's going to hit me*. As I turned my head to avoid the blow, she threw a punch that caught me in the side of my face. It rocked me right down to my feet. I managed to stay standing, but boy, could she hit.

Most of the mob were drunk or stoned on drugs, and that worked to my advantage. If a few of them had said, "Right, let's take this copper down," I would have been finished. But they weren't that organized.

I was running on adrenaline and survival instincts. *Stay up*, I told myself. *Stay on your feet*. I knew that if I fell down, I'd be dead.

Things began to run in slow motion. *Wham*, someone would hit me in the back of the head. I'd turn to fight back, and a blow would come from the other side. It would go quiet for a couple of seconds, and then someone else would hit me. I just kept swinging at anyone who came near, trying to drive them off.

This went on for about twenty minutes, and the longer it lasted, the more convinced I became that I was going to die. In the back of my mind, I was thinking about Police Constable Blakelock, who was working in London when the Tottenham riot broke out in 1985 and had been beaten to death by a mob. I was sure the same thing would happen to me.

As all this was happening, the kid in the back of the car began going berserk, kicking the windows of the car and trying to get out. He stuck his head out of the window and shouted, "Where's your God now, Graham?"

He'd heard that I was studying to be a priest, but still, it was quite a question to ask. We often say that God is with us when things are going well, but was God with me now? The great irony was that we were almost in the shadow of the church of St Peter and St Paul. A set of steps leading to the graveyard were less than a hundred feet from where I was.

I didn't have time to ponder theological questions. I was managing to stay up, but I was taking a lot of blows. I didn't know how long I would be able to keep fighting.

Whenever I got injured, it was always my police friend Roy Brown who had to go round and tell Kathy I was in hospital or that something had happened and I wouldn't be home. Standing there receiving the blows, I thought, *Roy is going to have to go round and break the news to her. Crumbs, Kathy's really going to be mad at me for being late.* Funny the things that run through one's mind.

Just when I was about to give up, the cavalry arrived. The first guy was a traffic officer named Neil Campbell, who saved me by driving his car right into the middle of the crowd. As soon as the mob heard the sirens – by now, police were coming from all corners – they took off. Eventually, three of them were arrested.

I was euphoric to be alive and still sky-high on adrenaline, so much so that I didn't realise how badly I was injured. I was just grateful to still be standing. The young offender was still in the backseat. Another officer hopped in the car with me, and we went straight down to the police station in Malton.

I can't believe now that I drove. When doing so, I kept looking at the lampposts and thinking, *Why are they leaning over like that?* My vision was blurry, and I couldn't focus. I didn't know it, but I had a concussion and likely some swelling in my brain. We made it to the station in Malton just when a call came in about a violent disturbance at a takeaway in a little town called Norton. Since all of the police from Malton were down in Pickering, the other officer and I got in the car and went to Norton to break up the disturbance.

By the time we returned from Norton, the effects of the adrenaline finally wore off. My head was pounding, my neck hurt, my hip was sore, and I was so bruised I could hardly move.

It also began to sink in how lucky I was to be alive. I realised how close I had come to dying, and I crumbled.

After the attack, I was completely and utterly shell-shocked. As a police officer, I had been beaten up and had suffered so many horrendous experiences that I just couldn't take it anymore. I had reached the end of my tether.

My body began to swell up from the bruises. Even something as simple as standing up brought excruciating pain. I couldn't hear out of my right ear, as the beating had caused permanent damage. I had a sore throat that wouldn't go away because a tumour was growing there, a result of the blows.

Even worse was the mental anguish. I would wake up in the middle of the night crying for no apparent reason. I once woke up with my head hanging out the window, gasping for air. Another night, I leapt out of bed, screaming and running naked through the house, then collapsing in a heap on the sofa downstairs. In my head, I was being beaten and was trying to get away. I'd have panic attacks anytime I saw a police uniform; I couldn't bear to have a uniformed policeman visit the house, not even one of my friends.

Kathy was my rock during this time. She listened patiently as I told the story over and over again, just trying to get it out of my system. As I got better, I realised that my mind had blocked out many of the details of that night. I began to remember more of them. Kathy would just listen and be there for me, not judging or criticizing when I was crying or freaking out in the middle of the night.

Roy Brown was a big help, as was another friend, Richard Hammond. But some of my friends, especially those on the force, didn't understand what was happening to me.

When I finally returned to work, I completely changed the way I policed. Before the attack, I had been an easygoing cop, but from then on, I was always ready for a fight. No one was ever going to get the jump on me again. I really wasn't well enough to be back on the force; I was just barely holding myself together.

One day while out on patrol, I saw two of the kids who'd been in the mob that night. I had a horrendous panic attack and had to pull the car to the side of the road. My heart was racing and felt like it was going to explode. I wanted to get back at them and had murderous thoughts of what I would do if I had the chance. But part of me knew that wouldn't do any good. After all, they weren't evil people; they were kids who got drunk and made a terrible mistake. I knew something about that from my days in London. I could have been one of those kids.

I felt like a fight was going on inside of me. One part of me wanted to get back at the kids, but the other part knew I had to forgive them. If I didn't, I would become bitter, and bitterness leads to unbalance and disease. It's one of the biggest killers we've got, bitterness, and I didn't want to go that way. I wanted to be free, and the only way to be free was to forgive.

One step towards learning to forgive was going to see a friend who was a counsellor. She had heard about the beating and rang me. "Look," she said, "come and see me." Like Kathy, she listened and helped me grapple with the idea of forgiveness.

I'm convinced that we can't go through life harbouring grudges against people; it's pointless. The Lord's Prayer, which is the prayer that Jesus taught his followers, says, "Forgive us our sins" – and this is from the Greek – "as we have already forgiven those who sin against us." Not "as we forgive those who sin against us," but "as we have *already* forgiven them." So we can't go to God until we have forgiven those who sin against us.

During this time, we had dear church friends from the local Methodist and Free churches who came and put their hands on me and prayed that God would heal me. Those prayers seeped into my body; it was as if God was permeating my body and breaking down the anger and pain, the bitterness and murderous thoughts festering inside me.

I remember the night when I could finally pray, "Lord Jesus, I forgive them for what they did to me. I forgive them, Lord." Then I started saying, "God, please forgive me. In the name of Jesus, please forgive me for harbouring murderous thoughts against them." When I did that, I started to feel free from the hatred I was carrying towards them. It didn't have a hold over me anymore.

One evening in the spring of 1994, I was on patrol along the high street in Pickering. It was midweek, and the street was quiet. I was working on my own, just trying to hold things together. I was still quaky inside, having nightmares and panic attacks. The trial for the three young men we'd arrested was coming up, and I was dreading having to relive the beating while giving my testimony.

Around ten o'clock, I looked up outside the Black Swan, and there they were, the three guys we'd arrested that night. It was just them and me. And I thought, *This is it. We're going to relive it, literally ten yards from where it all happened.*

I was reaching for my truncheon when one of them called out, "Graham, can we talk?"

Here we go, I thought.

"Look, Graham," one of them said, "we want you to forgive us. We're sorry for what we did. We didn't mean for it to happen; it just got out of hand."

I paused for a moment, taking it all in, and then said those three simple words: "I forgive you."

We stood there talking for a while. I'd been keeping tabs on them since the night of the attack and saw that they'd been trying to change their lives. They stopped getting drunk. They got jobs and girlfriends and were keeping out of trouble.

"I've seen what you've been like over the past year," I said. "The trial is coming up soon, and if I can help, I will."

"What do you mean?" they asked.

"I am prepared to tell the judge that this event has changed your life. If you want me to say something on your behalf, I'll do it." That last bit just came out.

During the trial at Crown Court, I had to read my statement to the judge. When I got to that question, "Where's your God now, Graham?" it was so quiet you could have heard a pin drop. I paused for a moment, and the judge rubbed his beard, as if to say, "Now, that's interesting."

I had pondered this question a lot since the beating and had come to realise that God had been right there with me that night in Pickering. If I had died then, because I'm a Christian, I would have gone straight to be with God. Obviously I survived, so I believe that God protected me. Either way, as a Christian, I win. No matter what I am going through, no matter what my circumstances are, Jesus is there. Some people will say that's a simplistic approach to life and faith. It may be, but it's what keeps me clinging to faith – sometimes by the skin of my teeth. After all, if the saying "Jesus loves me, this I know, for the Bible tells me so" is good enough for the theologian Karl Barth, it's good enough for me.

All three of the young men we'd arrested were convicted of violent disorder. In most cases, this conviction means going to prison for several years.

When the trial was over, I got a call to appear at the sentencing. The judge asked me to make a statement about the character of these three young men since the incident. I told him the truth, that this had been a watershed event for them, that it forced them to grow up and that they'd changed their lives. Based on my testimony, the judge decided to spare them prison.

A reporter was at the hearing, and the next day, the headline in the *Ryedale Gazette* read, "Heroic Officer Saves Assailants from Prison."

The day after that article was printed, I went to the police station and all of the coppers were silent. No one would speak to me, and I couldn't understand why. Then I got a call from a senior police officer. He told me what a disgrace I was and that I had betrayed my fellow officers. It felt worse than being beat up.

Some of my friends on the force told me the same thing. "Why did you do it, Graham?"

"Why didn't you just let them rot in prison?"

"This was your chance to get back at them; you could have put them away for a long time."

"You're just an idiot and a fool," one sergeant told me. "They'll be laughing at you behind your back."

But those lads had changed; they'd kept out of trouble and tried to make amends for what they'd done. They had asked me to forgive them, and as a Christian, that's what I had to do.

After that, my superiors kept an eye on me because they said I had lost my bottle – that I had lost my courage. I had forgiven those kids, they believed, because I was afraid. Once I stood up for those young men in court, I was seen as a coward who could not be trusted.

I didn't stay on the force long after that. I was still off sick much of the time, especially after I'd had to go to the hospital to have the growth removed from my throat. I was just not well physically or emotionally. My hip ached constantly, and walking for more than a few hundred feet was excruciating.

I can be very stubborn, and though I was completely shell-shocked, I still did the job. One afternoon I got called to a house where a man was holding his neighbour, a woman, at knifepoint. They'd had an affair, but she was married and was calling it off. He was threatening to kill her and then to kill himself. I went into the house and talked him down while two other officers snuck into the house from behind. When he heard them, he let her go, and I disarmed him. I might have been a wreck, but I was no "big, fat Jessie," despite what one of my sergeants said.

Even so, it all was just too much. Finally, one night in September 1995, I was out on patrol and realised I couldn't go on anymore. My friend Roy was on patrol that night in another car. We had a code word, 10-10, that meant we were going off duty. At the end of my shift, I called in to Roy and said, "I am going 10-10 forever." And that was that. I put the receiver down, then packed my stuff out of the police station and drove home.

The next morning, I rang up and told them I wasn't coming back. When my sergeant asked why, I said, "I've got a badly damaged hip, and my brain's gone." I was a broken man and simply couldn't do the job anymore.

The police force put me on sick leave while my consultant and my superiors discussed my future. The consultant diagnosed me with post-traumatic stress syndrome, which made me no longer fit to continue as a police officer. It took about three months for my retirement from the North Yorkshire Police to be finalized. By January 1995, this part of my life had come to an end.

10

DRACULA'S TOMB

For the first six months after leaving the police force, I did nothing. That took some getting used to, as the last six years of my police career had been a whirlwind of activity. When I wasn't working all hours of the night on patrol, I had been in theology class or serving as a priest-in-training on the weekends.

Though I had not realised it at the time, in Pickering I had been slowly changing into my father. He was absent during most of my childhood because of a relentless work schedule. Now Hannah and Abigail were growing up with a father too busy to make time for them. So during my recovery, I threw myself into the role of devoted father, trading car chases and visits to the morgue for walks to school and trips to the park. Leaving the force became a blessing in disguise. Kathy and the girls became my first priority.

No matter what else was happening – and, as I would soon learn, the life of a priest is filled with crises – my life at home took first priority. I didn't want to come home one day and find that my girls didn't know me, or even worse, hated me.

I prayed, I rested, I spent time with my girls, and I got well. Once the stress of police work was gone, my body and mind began to heal. It would take almost three years for life to return to some form of normality, but I was on the journey back. The journey still continues, and the events of my time on the police force still come back when the black dog of depression calls at my door.

After leaving the police force, I knew that sooner or later I would have to take my place in a parish ministry. The option of working a secular job and being a priest was closed. Despite my reservations, God had called me into ministry, and I knew it was time to answer that call. Several months into my new role as a hands-on father, Bishop Gordon Bates of Whitby rang and asked if I'd be interested in coming to his area. A new vicar, Reverend Michael Aisbitt, had been appointed to St Mary's Church in Whitby, and he needed a curate (an assistant). The job was mine if I wanted it. I told the bishop that I would pray about the offer and get back to him.

According to my consultant, I was well enough to go back to work. Not police work, but other, less stressful employment would be possible. After several long conversations with Kathy, and with God, I rang the bishop back and accepted the position.

St Mary's Church is steeped in history and sits high on the cliffs in Whitby, overlooking both the North Sea and the river Esk, which splits the town in two. A set of 199 stone steps leads from the riverfront to the graveyard that surrounds the church. Just behind the church, to the east, lay the ruins of the Whitby Abbey, which dates back to AD 1078. An earlier monastery, built around AD 650, was destroyed by the Vikings in AD 867.

I stepped out of St Mary's on my first day in Whitby to see a young man in his twenties coming up the steps, dressed in jeans and a black T-shirt and sporting a baseball cap.

"Hey Vic," he called out, as he reached the church. "Where's Dracula's tomb?"

"Son," I replied, "you've got more chance of finding Bugs Bunny in this graveyard than Dracula."

"But Bugs Bunny's not real," he said, a confused look coming over his face. The thought that Dracula was a figment of someone's imagination hadn't occurred to him.

Though my baseball-capped friend called me "Vicar," my real title was missioner. Being an Anglican priest, I'd wear a white clerical collar – affectionately known as a "dog collar" – so people would call me "Vicar" even though that wasn't my title. Technically, vicar is the title for a priest who runs a parish church. But as missioner, I was in charge of the mission hall – a large community centre by the river, complete with a kitchen and a coffee bar.

The mission had fallen into disuse, and very little was happening there; it was only open for an hour a day. Very quickly some volunteers and I opened it as a daily drop-in centre. We served tea and coffee, cakes and sandwiches, and the mission became a gathering place both for the people of the town and for visitors. We provided not only food but also a place for people to come and talk about God. We held church services at the chapel upstairs, but we also sprinkled conversations about God around the tables downstairs.

Life as a priest was very busy in Whitby, especially because we had four sites for worship services: St Mary's and St Hilda's, which Michael looked after, and the mission and St John's, which I had charge of. We traded off at times, and on some Sunday mornings, I would take the services at both St Mary's and St John's, with only fifteen minutes in between. So as soon as I'd shaken the last hand and waved the last worshiper off at St Mary's, I would rush back inside to grab my coat, and the race was on. Down the 199 steps on the east side of the Esk, being careful not to run over any stragglers, then dash madly across the bridge, then up another set of stairs (not 199, thankfully, but nearly) to the street that led to St John's. It was no good driving; there was no direct route across town, and even if I arrived on time, St John's had precious little parking.

For all intents and purposes, St John's was a dying church when Michael and I arrived. The church commission had it on a closure list, and there seemed little hope of reviving it. But little by little, the congregation began to grow. I suppose on one level it would have been easier if it hadn't – no more mad dashes across town from St Mary's, for one thing. One Sunday in particular after my crosstown dash, I arrived breathless with only a minute to spare and vowed to come up with some other solution.

The answer turned out to be a motorbike. As a clergyman, I'd taken a pay cut, from £20,000 down to £11,000, which meant the only class of car I could afford was a cheap and not very reliable one. I had found out about cheap cars that break down when I was driving to a village baptism – the rut in the middle of the road quickly relieved my car of its exhaust system. But a motorbike could go anywhere without the danger of losing its exhaust, so soon into my tenure in Whitby, I bought a small motorbike for getting around town. The sight of a priest riding up to the steps of a church on a motorbike, then bounding off and running inside is sure to draw a crowd.

St Mary's fame, if it can be called that, came after a little-known writer named Bram Stoker arrived in Whitby in 1890 to work on a novel about vampires. While reading accounts of vampire lore in the local library, he came across the name of a bloodthirsty count named Vlad Dracula from Transylvania, which he used as the name for his book. Stoker's setting came from the ruins of the Whitby Abbey and the eerie appearance of the town on dark nights when the fog rolls in. The wreck of the sailing ship *Demetrius*, which spilled its cargo of bodies in coffins into the North Sea, added another grisly detail for Stoker's imagination.

In the novel, Dracula comes ashore after the wreck of a ship called the *Demeter* and, assuming the shape of a black dog, climbs the 199 steps to St Mary's. In the church's graveyard, Dracula kills a young girl named Lucy, and later on, two vampire hunters wound the count on the sacred ground.

As an interesting aside, we liked to tweak the local legends and add some irony. During our New Year's Eve services, we would cook garlic bread in the coal stove that provided heat for the church.

Not long after arriving in Whitby, I learned that the town was obsessed with Dracula. Twice a year, a group of two to three thousand would-be vampires descended on the town for the Whitby Gothic Festival, a weekend-long celebration of Dracula and the occult. People came so regularly to look for Dracula's grave that we began asking for donations. Obviously, Dracula's grave didn't exist, but one of the rocks in the graveyard had a skull and crossbones carved into it, so if they wanted to make a donation to the church, I'd let them see the rock. For the most part, the vampires and I got along fine.

When the vampires and Goths came to town – dressed in black and wearing pale makeup to give them an undead appearance – we kept the mission open as a gathering spot. The Gothic weekend is known for raucous parties, so we wanted to provide a place of respite where people could come in and have a cup of tea or coffee instead of another pint or could join us for a worship service.

For the most part, the vampires and Goths were nice people with very strange ideas about spirituality. If they were serious about spirituality, and not just out for a laugh at the festival, we'd talk about immortality. That's the appeal of vampires – in the stories, vampires never die. I wanted these vampire followers to see that there was another way to live forever.

I used to get up and do unusual things during worship services to make them feel at ease. At the beginning of one sermon, for instance, I brought a stake and hammer with me into the pulpit and held them up, asking, "Who's next?"

They all laughed, but I had a deeper point I wanted to make with the stake. Dracula is killed in the Bram Stoker novel when a stake is driven through his heart, and he dies forever. But in true life, Jesus was killed on a cross of wood, a spear driven into his side, and he came back to live forever.

But relations between the church and the Gothic festival were not always cordial. One October evening, festival organizers wanted to hold a torch-lit processional up the stairs leading to St Mary's. Whether or not Dracula was buried there, they wanted to have a ceremony on the church grounds. But that's where we drew the line. Thankfully, they backed off.

Life went on, and the daily rounds went on as usual. During the day, I put the horrors of policing in Pickering behind me, but every few months, I was still tortured in my dreams. The nightmares were nearly always the same, as if a videotape of the beating were playing over and over again. I was back on the high street in Pickering, the blows hammering down around me. I would try to run, but the mob, faceless and dark, would not let me go. Voices screamed out, and I was sure that this time the mob would kill me. As I fell to the ground, the mob began stomping on me, wracking my body in pain. I screamed and rolled on the ground, trying to escape the boots as they battered my body. Then suddenly, Kathy would be by my side, telling me it was only a dream and that I was safe at home.

On nights like this, I would go downstairs and pace the house, convinced that there was no God – that everything I believed was a lie. The reality of the nightmare, of being so close to dying, overwhelmed me.

"Please, Jesus," I would pray, "just be with me."

And then suddenly, I thought, *At least I have Jesus*. No matter what I feel, I have Jesus. That thought, that Jesus was with me and understood my suffering, sustained me. As a Christian, I knew that God was not distant, that he became human in Jesus and suffered for our sakes. The Hebrew prophet Isaiah describes the Messiah as "a man of sorrows, and familiar with suffering." And that's what Christians believe Jesus was. "Surely he took up our infirmities and carried our sorrows," Isaiah wrote, "yet we considered him stricken by God, smitten by him, and afflicted. But he was pierced for our transgressions, he was crushed for our iniquities; the punishment that brought us peace was upon him, and by his wounds we are healed" (Isaiah 53:4–5).

Some Christians believe that people will be happy and prosper when they find Jesus and that suffering is a sign of sin. But that's rubbish. Look at Dietrich Bonhoeffer, the German theologian who is one of the greatest Christian minds of our age. He wasn't very successful or happy; he was killed by the Nazis. And he wasn't the first Christian martyr; all twelve of Jesus' disciples were killed. We can know God and be doing God's will and still suffer horrible things. But God remains with us.

A priest is often with people at the most terrible moments of life – when a loved one has died, when their marriage is falling apart or when the doctors give a grim diagnosis. In those circumstances, a prosperity gospel is no help at all. What people need is a listening ear and someone to walk through the pain and suffering with them. If I had come to the priesthood having never suffered myself, I would have about as much use as a chocolate fireguard. Any platitudes I might have learned at theological college would have melted straight away.

St Mary's was about to be on television, and I was about to have my fifteen minutes of fame. Or infamy, as it turned out.

In the mid-1990s, ITV put on a television magazine programme in which it broadcast live Sunday morning worship services from a variety of towns, from 10:00 a.m. to noon. The churches in Whitby were asked to organize a seaside service for July 1997 that included all of the Christian groups in town – Anglicans, Methodists, evangelicals, charismatics, you name it. Under ordinary circumstances, as the vicar of the Anglican church, Michael Aisbitt would have chaired the committee planning the service. But he was going to be out of town, so the job fell to me.

As town missioner, I was asked by the other committee members to preach the sermon. ITV had given us a broadcast date but no specific instructions about the theme of the sermon. So I planned to speak about the cross of Christ, about how Jesus died to forgive us our sins. But I wanted to make the crucifixion real. Instead of having it glorified and sanitized, I wanted to present it as true to life as possible. It was a dreadful event. Jesus was beaten so much that even his own mother couldn't recognize him, the Roman soldiers drove spikes through his arms and feet, and when the soldiers hoisted Jesus in the air, every breath became excruciating – he had to push off with his feet, which were nailed to the post, to lift his head and gasp for air.

When it came time for a rehearsal, we set up by the shore, and the television producers and crew watched a run-through of the service. Afterwards one of the producers thanked me for the sermon and asked if he could have a written copy. I don't usually use a written sermon; I preach from my notes. But I went home, typed out the sermon and faxed it to him.

The next morning, the phone rang. It was one of the directors of religious broadcasting for ITV. After a few minutes of small talk, he got to the main point.

"Would you mind changing your sermon?"

"Why's that?" I asked.

"It's too violent."

"But it's about the crucifixion."

"It's too violent."

"But the crucifixion *was* violent. And it's a rather important part of Christianity."

"Yes," he replied, "but I think it's going to be too violent for television."

"Well, I'm sorry," I said, "but this is the gospel. This is how it happened. And this is what I'm going to preach."

"Couldn't you preach on something else?" he asked. "What about boats?"

As we would be worshiping by the shore, he insisted that boats were a sensible alternative to my "violent sermon."

"Jesus didn't die on a boat," I responded. "He died on a cross. So that's what I'll preach about."

Once it was clear that he wasn't going to change my mind, he ended the conversation. An hour later, the phone rang again. This time it was the bishop.

"Graham," he said, "an old friend's been in touch with me, and he's not very happy about the sermon you'll be preaching on television. Could you send me a copy of it?"

"Yes, Bishop," I said, "I'd be happy to fax it to you."

After he received the copy, he called me back and said that he didn't find any problems with the sermon. On the request of the TV producer, the bishop asked me to change the sermon, but I think he realised it was pointless to get me to change my mind.

The upshot was that ITV refused to film the sermon, so Michael and I decided to pull out of the programme. We were not going to compromise the gospel for the sake of getting on television. The crucifixion of Jesus is a central part of Christianity and can't be set aside. Think about this another way: can you imagine a television producer asking a Muslim imam to delete some of the details of the life of Mohammed? Or asking a Buddhist monk to change the message of Buddha – who taught that all life is about suffering – to make it more palatable? Or telling a Hindu priest to tidy up the life of Krishna for television? I can't imagine a Muslim, Buddhist or Hindu going along with that. And neither should a Christian.

The programme went ahead without us on 27 July 1997. One television crew set up on the grounds of the Whitby Abbey, just to the east of St Mary's, while another went down to the seaside to film the service. Unfortunately, the television crew at the Abbey had made a small but significant error – they neglected to account for the bells at St. Mary's. Those bells were chimed every Sunday morning before church services, regardless of whether a television programme was being broadcast live next door.

At 10:00 a.m., just as the presenter, Gloria Hunniford, came on the air, the bells started to ring. When all the baffles are up, the bells of St Mary's are extremely loud; they can be heard ten miles out to sea. A few hundred feet away, the sound can be deafening.

Later we saw a videotape of the broadcast. Poor Gloria attempted valiantly to conduct a live TV show whilst the bells of St Mary's rattled away. At one point, she turned straight to the camera and said something like, "I think they are trying to tell us something."

Things were no better down by the river, where a pulpit had been set up. They had found someone else to preach, but all the viewers could hear were the bells going *ding dong, ding dong.*

The whole incident proved that God has a sense of humour. That night, a reporter from one of the national newspapers rang me. He'd heard about the sermon and wanted to get my side of the story. And the next morning, the *Sun* ran a news item – "Vicar Quits TV Service after Row" – detailing how my sermon contained "violent language" that "might upset people watching the seaside service." Never mind that at the time, the network offered a nightly dose of sex, drugs, murder and infidelity.

Once the *Sun* ran the story, the editor of the *Whitby Gazette* rang, offering to run the sermon – just as I gave it – in the paper. They ran it on a full two-page spread. The *Gazette* is mailed out around the world to people who have connections to Whitby, and the sermon was eventually picked up and duplicated in newspapers in Wyoming, Canada and New Guinea, billed as "the sermon that was too violent for TV." People wanted to read the sermon because it had been banned. If it hadn't been, it would have been on TV once and faded away. The television network was outnumbered by God.

God always seemed to be surprising us in Whitby. Sometimes we Christians get discouraged when our congregations are small, and we wonder if all the work is worth it. But we keep showing up faithfully, because we never know when God is up to something.

Some of his work in Whitby was seemingly routine, without fireworks. One Sunday at St Mary's, I noticed a woman dressed in hiking gear – boots, long trousers, a jumper and hat – with a backpack sitting on the pew next to her. During the coffee time, we chatted. She was on a long-distance walk, and as she came into the main part of Whitby, she heard the bells ringing. She was looking for a place to rest for a few minutes, so she came into the church. During the service, something stirred inside of her, so afterwards she asked if I would pray for her. Kathy and I went with her into the chancel, and there we knelt and prayed together. Nothing earth-shattering happened, and afterwards she bid us goodbye and went on her way. But she met God, in a quiet but meaningful way.

Another day, a woman stopped by the mission, desperately looking for someone to pray with her. She lived seventy miles away and had come by bus to Whitby, climbing the steps to St Mary's and hoping that God would speak to her there. But she hadn't felt anything and left despondent. While waiting for the bus home, she sat in the mission and had some coffee. Kathy and one of her friends were working in the mission that day, and they sat with the woman, listening to her story. She was dealing with a crisis in her life – Kathy never told me the details – and she asked for prayer. The three of them went upstairs to the chapel and prayed together for an hour. The time for the bus came, and as she bid Kathy and her friends goodbye, she said, "I was looking for God, and I didn't find him at the church. But I found him here." Makes me think of what Jesus told his followers, that whenever two or more people are gathered in his name, he would be there with them. As he was that day in the mission.

The mission also attracted a fair share of interesting characters. One of my favourites was a tramp who was on a continuous tour of Britain. He would always arrive in Whitby about May and would be extremely thin, as if he'd gone for weeks without eating a good meal. He came to the mission every day, and we'd sit with him and listen to his stories. Over the summer, he'd eat everything in sight, and so by September, he'd be so fat he couldn't button his coat. It was like he was a bear, coming in and getting fattened up for the winter. He'd go off, and we wouldn't see him for months until the next May, when he'd return, again slimmed down.

Life followed a pattern of births, marriages and deaths. When death came too early, my faith was tested to its limits.

The funeral was on New Year's Eve, and St Mary's was full to overflowing. A young man had died at Christmas, and nearly a thousand people had gathered to pay their last respects. He'd been out walking along the cliffs that overlook the sea when he slipped on some ice and fell to his death. It was tragic to see such a great kid snatched away so suddenly, one who enjoyed life and came from a kind, loving family.

When I was a police officer, I often tried to give comfort as best I could to those who were grieving. But I always had a job to do; information to collect and difficult questions to ask. And I couldn't pray with a parent who'd lost a child or speak about God. But as a priest, I had the privilege of praying with those in grief and helping them say goodbye to their loved ones.

When I met with this young man's family to plan the funeral, they asked if they could play some taped pop music during the ceremony. I agreed, so the family and friends filed in to the sounds of his favourite rock band echoing through the church. When I stood to preach, I saw a sea of young faces. As a priest, I decided very early on never to say the words "the Lord giveth and the Lord taketh away." That's simply not true. God doesn't cause a young man to fall from a cliff or a mother to die of cancer. Sickness and disease take away. Human frailty takes away. But God doesn't.

When it came time in the service for the prayers, I was surrounded by an incredible silence. What struck me most was the sight of his family being so brave, genuine and united, and all around him so many young people who loved their son. It was one of those moments that will never leave me.

Three weeks later, I had to take the funeral of another young man, this one a lad who had died of a drug overdose. His funeral was in marked contrast to the one earlier, as only a few people came, including the dealer, who sat five or six rows in front of the pulpit. I had taken several funerals like this since coming to Whitby, and it always burned me up inside. The dealers tended to be older guys in their thirties who were willing to sell somebody's life down the river for ten quid. And that's what this dealer had done; he sold this young kid the drugs that had killed him. Now he had the nerve to sit in church without a hint of remorse.

When it came time for the sermon, I started by saying that this young man hadn't died but was murdered by the dealer who gave him the stuff. The dealer bowed his head as if to deflect attention away from himself. But I wasn't having any of it. The pulpit at St Mary's is set about six feet above the congregation, and I wanted to jump out of the pulpit, grab him and beat him up. I was so angry that he had destroyed this young kid's life by filling him full of drugs.

The sight of a mad, ginger-haired, seventeen-stone priest crashing down from on high might have been enough to put the fear of God in the dealer. But certainly the dead boy's parents, not to mention the bishop, would have frowned on a leap from the pulpit. I would have to leave vengeance in God's hands.

Thankfully, not all funerals are sombre affairs. In Whitby, the tradition was for the coffin to be placed into the ground, the priest to give the blessing, and then the family members to tip in a bottle of the person's favourite drink. Sometimes it was a Guinness, but more often than not, it was whiskey.

At one gravesite, the family opened a huge bottle of scotch and passed it around. Each of them had a swig before passing the bottle to me. Not wanting to offend, I took a swig and passed it back. Then one of the dead man's brothers poured the remains of the bottle into the grave. As several people lit cigarettes, I couldn't help but hope that no one would throw their ashes into the grave, or we'd have had a cremation.

People would also throw money into the grave, I suppose thinking that the deceased would have money in the afterlife. I remember one funeral in particular when we'd buried a young man who died. His friends came up and began tossing coins in, and suddenly the coffin was bombarded with money. The banging and clattering of it sounded like steel rain falling down on the kid's coffin. I half expected him to call out from inside the box, "Cut that out. Don't you know you I'm trying to sleep in here?"

The ground around the Whitby churchyard was often saturated with water. So it wasn't uncommon for the bottom of a dug-out grave to fill up with water. All of our coffins were made of laminated woods, usually oak or pine, and if there was enough water, the coffin would float. For one older gentleman's family, this was more than they could bear. After the coffin was lowered into the grave with a splash and began bobbing up and down, I heard a wave of giggles followed by full belly laughs from the family.

After a few minutes, I asked one of the man's sons what was so funny.

"Well," he said with a grin, "he couldn't swim."

II

ADVENTURES OF A
VILLAGE VICAR

I t was time for a cup of tea. We had just moved to the vicarage in Cloughton, a small village on the edge of the North
Yorkshire Moors, just north of Scalby. Kathy had spent the
day unpacking boxes and rearranging furnishings while I was
out visiting and attending church meetings. After five years
in Whitby, I had been made vicar of Cloughton in August of
1999 and was given care of three churches: St Mary's Church
in Cloughton, St Hilda's in Ravenscar, and St John the Baptist
in Stainton Dale.

Cloughton is a linear village, with houses lining either side
of a main road. It used to be called Clockton because a bell
tower in the village used to call travellers down off the moors.
The North Yorkshire Moors, a series of hills, woods and wild,
open fields, were a really scary place to be. Bears and wolves
and other wild animals roamed free, and it was not somewhere
to wander about at night.

It was nearly 9:00 p.m., and the girls – including Lydia,
our newest addition, who was born in 1998 just before we left
Whitby – were asleep. Kathy put on the kettle for tea and sent
me out to get milk. Still wearing my clerical shirt and dog collar, I climbed in our aging Vauxhall Cavalier, thanked God

when the car started and drove through the graveyard that surrounded the vicarage. Cloughton is a small village – fewer than three hundred people – with no stores open at that time of night, so I headed towards Scalby.

Something seemed wrong from the moment I pulled alongside the newsagent on the outskirts of town. The shop was in the Newlands, not far from the pub where my father had worked, and there was no movement inside, no sign of the clerk. My old policeman's bones told me that something was out of place.

As I walked towards the door, two kids in their twenties came running out from behind the counter. One of them had a bag in his hands. They had robbed the shop and were making a getaway. Instinctively, I grabbed the kid nearest to me and threw him to the ground while the other one ran off. Before he knew what had hit him, I grabbed him in an armlock and got on top of him.

"Right," I said, "you're nicked."

When he screwed his head around to look at me, I could see his pupils were widely dilated, a sign that he was high on drugs. He stared at me. "Who the f--- are you?" He just couldn't understand why some mad vicar had grabbed him and thrown him to the floor.

Just then the clerk came out and told me the police were on the way.

"Thanks," he said, before going back inside.

A moment after I nabbed the kid, I could hear sirens in the background, and after a minute or two, the police constables arrived.

One of them recognized me from my days on the force. "Graham," he said, "we didn't know it was you."

The clerk had told the police that some crazed vicar had tackled one of the thieves. The constables hauled away this poor kid, who still couldn't believe he'd been arrested by a priest.

When Lydia turned a year old, Kathy took her in to the doctors for a whooping-cough immunization. Most children tolerate the shot with little side effects, but Lydia reacted violently. She developed a horrible case of eczema, first around the spot where she'd had the injection, and then spreading over her whole body. At the worst moments, the skin would dry up and drop off her body like scales. The doctors gave us several treatments for her, but they were ineffective. We turned to God in prayer, and even that seemed to fail us. The skin condition persisted for years. We prayed and prayed and sought doctor after doctor, to no avail.

At the worst point of her illness, when I was ready to give up, Lydia put her hand on mine one day as we were praying. "Don't worry, Daddy," she said. "Jesus is here." My eyes filled with tears as I realised that she was right. No matter what we go through, Jesus is there with us. Sometimes we don't see him, but he is there with us.

I knew that God would help Lydia but didn't know how. All else seemed to have failed, and I was sinking into a deep depression over the whole thing. Funny that at the time, *Shadowmancer* was taking off and becoming a great success. But I was worried about my little girl.

One day Kathy was praying, and she felt she had a word from God. All she could sense were the words "A time is coming and has come." She felt that God was saying Lydia would be healed. From that day on, Lydia's condition began to improve. Slowly the skin began to heal and the sores to disappear. Lydia began to change too. No longer did she hold her hands as if they would break open with the slightest movement. Gone were the constant scratching and terrible itching that had plagued her life. And we didn't live in a state of paranoia, wondering if a cat would stray into the garden and cause her to be ill with the allergy. We could go on the beach, in the snow or to visit friends. Her sleep was getting better too; Kathy no longer had to spend the night wrapping Lydia in wet bandages and covering her flaking skin in creams.

A time was coming and *had* come – our daughter was being given back to us.

When I accepted the job in Cloughton, I thought I was going to three fully functioning churches, small though they may have been. But whenever my clergy colleagues heard that one of the churches was in Ravenscar, they'd get a quizzical look on their faces. "Ravenscar?" they'd ask, as if they misheard me. "Are you sure you're going to Ravenscar?" Despite my repeated enquiries, none of them would say what was wrong.

Soon after arriving, I learned that St Hilda's was not exactly fully functional. The congregation was small, only about five or six people. After the service, I took a tour of the building and found that one of the doors was locked. No matter, I'd take a look behind that door after the next weekend's service.

But the next weekend, the door was still locked. This time I got the church warden to come with me.

"What's behind this door?" I asked her.

"That's the church hall," she said.

"Can I have a look?

She said, "Well, you can ... " and then hesitated.

"Right," I said. "Open the door please."

She unlocked the door and revealed a scene of devastation. The walls were literally falling in. I stepped over to one of them and saw that the plaster had bubbled away from the brickwork and was barely hanging on. The floorboards were rotten, and there were holes where parts of the floor had caved. Everywhere I looked, I saw rotting wood. St Hilda's was a beautiful church that had been neglected over the years and was now crumbling to pieces.

I looked over at the warden. "Right," I said. "We've got to keep this locked up at all times."

The warden and I sat and had a chat about the condition of the church. About six months earlier, the remaining four members of the congregation had met with the vicar to discuss closing the church. They were literally bankrupt. With four people, they didn't have the finances or the wherewithal to keep the church open. Somehow this information hadn't reached me in Whitby before my arrival.

The church had other problems as well. It had no working heating system, so during the winter months, parishioners used portable propane heaters during services to make the old stone church bearable.

In the weeks that followed, we had an estimate made of the repairs needed. The news was daunting – we needed £200,000 to make the church functional again. With a congregation of just four people, it'd take fifty years or more to raise that much money. Overwhelmed, we did the only thing we could do: we fasted and prayed. There's a long Christian tradition of fasting during times of great need, and this certainly fit the bill.

From a building standpoint, things were better at St John the Baptist in Stainton Dale. The congregation was small there as well, with only six to ten people attending weekend services. Although the church building was in good repair, relations between the Christians in the village were strained.

A Methodist church had always been in Stainton Dale, and this had upset the Anglicans. So the Anglicans built a church a hundred yards away. Over the years, however, both churches had dwindled in size. One Sunday morning, I came to the village for a service and observed six cars parked outside the Methodist church and six cars parked outside the Anglican church. That Sunday, we sang the same hymns and each had a communion service to worship the one true God but in two separate buildings. It was just crazy to have eight people in one church and six people in another. If we got the two groups together, we could have a really good service.

I rang the Methodists' part-time minister, who looked after the churches in the area. Would he be open to holding combined services? He agreed to consider it, and over the next few months, we began making plans for a local ecumenical project.

To begin with, we alternated services between St John's and the Methodist chapel. As we began meeting together, interesting things began to happen. We started out with fourteen people, and before too long, twenty, then thirty, and then forty, people meeting for worship.

Not long after the combined services began in Stainton Dale, I stopped in a café near Ravenscar for a cup of coffee. A woman who lived nearby was there, and we struck up a conversation. She was a lovely older lady who never came to St Hilda's but knew who I was. Over the next hour, we drank coffee and talked about God and life after death. She'd not been well and seemed eager to talk. At the end of the conversation, she went her way and I went mine.

We never met again, and she died a few months later. Never once in the conversation did the condition of the Ravenscar church come up, but she left us £200,000 pounds in her will. Exactly what we needed to repair St Hilda's church.

Being a vicar is a tough job. People think it's easy, because they think vicars only work one day a week. But it's actually very demanding. I was in charge of three churches, so a typical Sunday would include services at 8:00, 10:00 and 11:30 in the morning and 6:30 in the evening, with a couple of baptisms in the afternoon. The rest of the week would be taken up with parish activities, such as going to people's homes, participating in community events, taking weddings and funerals and visiting the sick in hospital.

Being a Church of England vicar is different than being a minister of one church. Some Protestant churches have a minister who cares solely for one congregation, but a C of E vicar cares for the whole parish, whether or not they come to church. Everyone in the parish is the vicar's parishioner, whether Christian, Jew, Muslim, Hindu or Wiccan. The vicar's job is to minister to the whole community, no matter who they are or what they believe.

Grace took me to places where some Christians might not want to go. Allan, a retired consultant surgeon, started coming to church about the same time I arrived at St Mary's, and before long, he started what he called the "Sunday afternoon prayer meeting." After the eleven-thirty service, Allan and some friends from church would have a cup of coffee and then go down the road to the pub for a drink before lunch. He invited me to go along.

Going to the pub after church became a weekly tradition. I'd sometimes be there in my cassock, drinking a Coke along with Allan, the church treasurer and as many of the others who wanted to come along. It was a chance to talk and have a drink together before Sunday lunch.

Some of my evangelical friends think that Jesus would be outside the pub saying, "You mustn't go in there!" But I think hanging out in the pub with his mates is just what Jesus would have done. The Pharisees would have stood outside and pointed their fingers, saying, "Look at that Jesus. He's in there with all that lot!" But Jesus told his followers to be salt and light in the world, therefore I want to go where the people are. If we have too much salt in a meal, we can't eat it. So we need to spread ourselves thinly in the world and affect as much of it as we possibly can. When we Christians stay grouped together in church, like a big pile of salt, we can poison ourselves.

Life as a village vicar was never dull. I earned the title of "John Wayne, the cowboy vicar," at Christmastime. Every year, about two or three days before Christmas, some hundred members of the local pony club go out Christmas carolling on horseback, and as vicar, I was expected to go along. All the money they collected went to charity.

Growing up on a council estate, I'd never ridden a horse as a kid and had ridden only once or twice as an adult. One of the club members brought along a spare horse for me and gave me a quick lesson. All I had to do, he assured me, was hold on; the horse knew what to do. "You'll be fine, Vicar," he said as I climbed into the saddle. Everyone else mounted up and set off for the first house.

The moment the other horses moved, my horse pricked up his ears. His whole body went tense, as if a spring were coiling up. I knew something was wrong but didn't have time to think before the horse broke into a gallop. What no one had told me is that this horse used to be the lead horse for the foxhunt, so it never wanted to be behind any other horses.

As the rest of the carollers watched, their vicar was catapulted to the front of the pack, bouncing up and down while hanging on for dear life. The horse would stand perfectly still while we carolled, but the minute we stopped singing, he took off like a rocket.

It was one of the joys and challenges of being a vicar – I had to take part in all of these strange events. Whether it was the mother's union afternoon tea session, mad foxhunting with

rifles, or the pony-club carolling, it was all part of the rich tap-
estry of being a parish priest.

After the Easter services in the spring of 2000, Kathy and I
spent several days on holiday in London, our first real break
since coming to Cloughton the previous summer. When we got
home, Kathy went into town to do some shopping, and I went
outside to work in the garden. The vicarage was set in the middle of a graveyard, bordered by a field that turned into woods.

I was on my knees weeding when I heard a faint cry, high
and shrill, coming from one of the nearby trees. It sounded like
a bird was injured and in pain. A number of cats roamed around
the vicarage, and I feared one of them had pounced on the bird.
If it was injured, the bird would likely die, but since I hate to
see an animal suffer, I decided to go investigate.

A baby crow lay at the bottom of the tree, covered in lice.
When I picked it up, the lice ran up my arms and bit them.
They were horrendous things, quick and difficult to dislodge.

What now? I wondered.

We had a cage in the vicarage for transporting our dog, and
with a little work, it made a suitable birdcage. I put a little stand
inside the cage and made a nest of twigs and leaves, thinking
that this would make a comfortable place for the bird to die.

I got a boiled egg from the kitchen, mashed it, and using an
empty syringe, sprayed it in the crow's mouth. The crow settled
down, contented after its meal. About six hours later, the baby
crow began crying, and this time I gave it some chopped-up
meat. This became a regular practice, like having another baby
in the house. Low and behold, the crow didn't die; it just kept
growing and growing.

We named the crow Mark, and it became a family pet.
Mark's left wing was badly broken in the fall from the tree,

and it had a deformed right foot, so it would never fly. Instead, Mark became my constant companion in the vicarage. He followed me around the garden and sometimes sneaked into the house and pulled off the wallpaper. The crow stayed outside in the daytime, and we'd bring it inside at night. At teatime, Mark would sit at the back door and wait to be fed, wings flapping frantically as "Daddy" came to feed it. Because I found the crow when it was so young, I believe Mark looked on me as a parent.

Mark used to chase the dog around the garden; he loved to play games. He would bring us a stone to throw. Just like a dog with feathers instead of fur, he'd hop after the stone, scoop it up in his beak and bring it back, waiting happily for us to throw it again.

When I was gardening, Mark would follow me around. I would dig the garden, and he would eat the worms. I think he believed I was digging the worms up just for him.

Though our finances had improved slightly when we came to Cloughton, we were still close to the edge. Three young children grow fast, and supporting a family of five on £16,500 a year meant money was a constant irritation. We were never down and out, however, and Kathy and I tried our best to spare the children from knowing that we were poor. They always had clothes for school, and we made sure that birthdays and Christmas were special occasions. We shopped at the cheapest shops, drove a really bad, secondhand car, and Kathy and I went without. We were never overdrawn because we were always very careful, but if the car went wrong, we were stuck.

We always used to save up five hundred pounds for Christmas to make sure we could buy the presents, food and everything else. But often something would go wrong with the car, and we'd end up spending the Christmas money on repairs. During those times, the church was good to us. If the car went wrong at Christmas, sometimes we'd get a poor cheque to get us through.

My prize possession, and the only thing of value we owned, was a Yamaha XV1100 Virago motorcycle. During my years at Whitby, I'd saved my petrol allowance to pay for the Yamaha, along with the proceeds from the sale of my smaller motorcycle. All black metal and chrome, the motorbike looked much like the chopper-style Harley-Davidson that Hell's Angels drive. It had a low-slung seat and high handlers and 1100 CCs of grunt for an engine. I called it my "smiling machine" because it made me feel good every time I got on it. The bike would go anywhere, up hills and over the moors, making it perfect for pastoral visits. The Yamaha used less petrol than the car and was more reliable.

Roaring across the moors perched on the motorbike in my leather jacket, with the wind whipping through my hair, was as close to a midlife crisis as I got. I obeyed the 30-mile-per-hour speed limits completely, as people would likely be nearby, but on the moor, I was less scrupulous about the 70-mile-per-hour zones.

Just outside of Cloughton was a stretch of road where I could race the bike at 100 or perhaps 110 miles per hour before braking as the road went downhill and into a hairpin turn. There's nothing like hurtling downhill with the sound of the motorcycle in your ears and banking into the bend of the road. I learned quickly not to get too far into the middle of the road, for fear of getting my head taken off by someone coming around the other way. The essential thing was to watch for potholes; hitting a pothole at 110 miles per hour would be a nasty experience.

Little did I know that I would soon part company with my beloved motorbike, which would take me in a completely new direction in life.

One thing I didn't learn in theological college is how to do an exorcism. In medieval times, it was a capital offence not to be able to deliver someone from an evil spirit; if vicars couldn't do it, they were put to death. Nowadays, exorcisms are a forgotten part of Christian ministry.

First in Whitby and later in Cloughton, I began to do "house blessings," which sounds much nicer than the word *exorcisms*. The best way to describe them is as a kind of spiritual spring cleaning. In the ten years I was in parish ministry, I did at least a hundred of them. Of course, my first encounter was our own impassioned prayer in our snug cottage in Scalby in 1984.

The word *exorcist* brings up all kinds of connotations, most involving heads spinning 360 degrees and buckets of green vomit, based on the movie from the seventies. None of the house blessings I did were anything like that.

Perhaps the best way to explain a house blessing is to think of a videotape. If we pull apart a videotape, all we'll see are yards and yards of magnetic tape. On that tape are tiny, invisible electromagnetic images. Under the right circumstances, those images will come alive and begin to move.

Houses and other buildings can be like a videotape. We human beings give off energy, which we cannot see and cannot feel, yet this energy has the ability to impregnate the wood and stone, bricks and doors, walls and ceilings. We can experience this when we're in a house where there's just been an argument; the tension is still in the air. If that tension is not dispelled, it builds up year after year, and the house can become a very unpleasant place.

We can experience the opposite in the house of a beloved grandmother or some other loved one whose presence seems to fill their home even when they aren't there. We can also feel it in a church that has been prayed in for many years; those prayers seem to vibrate in the very stones of the building, creating a holy atmosphere. St Mary's in Cloughton, St Mary's in Whitby, and St Peter and St Paul in Pickering all had very holy atmospheres because they were places of regular, committed, deep prayer.

In a house blessing, I would ask God to replace any negative emotion in a building with the Holy Spirit. I would come to the house, talk with the people who lived there about what had been going on, and then we'd pray together, inviting the Holy Spirit to come in.

Sometimes people would report spiritual activity – things like objects moving, doors slamming, footsteps wandering across the landing upstairs, things going missing, objects being thrown around the room, disturbances of sleep – but those things were very rare. Usually what someone thought was a poltergeist was actually a leaky radiator that knocked in the night.

A house blessing can be like a breath of fresh air. People would say that their house felt better, that the central heating was working now where they always felt cold before or that the manifestations in the house had stopped. That was the most important thing, that whatever negative mood had settled over the house was lifted and the people could live in peace.

House blessings could get rid of spooks but not foxes. A fox got Mark the crow on a summer evening while Kathy and I were out celebrating our anniversary. We had gone to Scarborough to see Alan Ayckbourn play at the Stephen Joseph Theatre and did not get home until eleven o'clock. It was July, and at that time of year in Cloughton, it is still light outside.

Most nights we brought Mark inside and put him in his cage in the early evening. But that night we'd left him outside, and a fox crept into the back garden and ate him. All that was left were a pair of feathers in the centre of the garden, although later we found one of his feet.

After I became a vicar, Hannah, Abigail and Lydia would make me do a service when a pet died. I have buried many hamsters, a few rabbits and a couple of cats in my time but never before a crow. Mark was an incredible bird that brought me much joy, and I was deeply sad when he was killed.

"Vengeance is mine," says the Lord, and thankfully I didn't have to wait long to find mine. It was three in the morning when I heard a mad scream coming from behind the vicarage. Something was in my chicken hut. Again.

A few weeks earlier, I'd come home in the afternoon to find all of our chickens lying dead in the back garden, their heads bitten off and a few of their bodies gnawed to bits. A fox had broken into the chicken hut and killed them all. It was a nightmare.

We got the chickens soon after moving to Cloughton. When I was growing up, one of my favourite programmes had been *The Good Life*, about a couple named Tom and Barbara, who quit the rat race and started growing and raising all their own food in the back garden. After seeing that show, I'd always wanted to keep chickens and have fresh eggs every morning. So soon after moving into the vicarage, I bought some chicken wire and set up a chicken hut under the trees. I bought some hens and every morning went out and collected the eggs while they were still warm and fresh.

Now a fox had come and killed off our lovely chickens. Undaunted, I went to the hardware store and bought more chicken wire to repair the damage. Once the chicken run was repaired, we bought new chickens and put them inside it. I went to sleep dreaming of fresh eggs for breakfast.

About three in the morning, the chickens started squawking, going absolutely crazy. I leapt out of bed, pulling open the curtains. It was midsummer, so the back garden was illumined in twilight. A male fox stalked back and forth outside the chicken hut, looking for a way in. The hens were scampering for cover and squawking as loudly as they could.

I started banging on the window to try to scare the fox off. It didn't move. I opened the window, leaned my head out and yelled at it, and still it didn't move away. As I yelled and banged, the fox turned its head towards me, as if to say, "Look, you're up there, I am down here. What are you going to do to me from up there?"

Dressed only in a pair of underpants, I ran downstairs into the kitchen. The kitchen door was a glass door, and I could see the fox still out in the back garden, trying to get the hens. I opened up the back door and shouted at the fox.

"Get away from my chickens! Get out of there!"

Still the fox stayed put.

By now, I was furious. I ran into the garden like a madman, screaming bloody murder. All the fox did was walk away. As I ran towards it, from about forty feet away, the fox sauntered to the fence, casually leapt over it and sat on the other side. The fox was taunting me, I was sure of it – "You can't catch me, you fat old vicar."

Infuriated, I dashed to the fence, leapt over it and chased the fox into the woods at the edge of our neighbour's garden, screaming like a banshee.

Once I was sure the fox had run off, I called after it, "And don't you come back either."

About then, I realised that I was standing in my next-door neighbour Suzan's garden, practically naked and screaming at the top of my lungs. Clearly a dodgy situation to be in. I beat a hasty retreat towards home.

As I reached the edge of the drive that ran between Suzan's house and the vicarage, a pair of headlights appeared. The milk van was coming. As the lights and the rattle of milk bottles drew closer, I dove into the bushes beside my neighbour's house.

There was no time for a mad dash to my house, nor did I cherish explaining to the driver why I was sneaking out from behind my neighbour's house, half naked, in the middle of the night.

So I hid. I crouched behind the bush, held my breath and prayed he wouldn't see me. The van passed me in the bushes and stopped at the back of the house. The driver got out, left several bottles of milk on the neighbour's porch and climbed back in the van. As he backed out, the driver leaned out the window of the van and waved. "Morning, Vicar," he said, in a cheery voice.

My early morning adventures with the fox made for interesting breakfast conversation. Kathy nearly fell over laughing as I recounted being trapped in the bushes by the milk van. After we had a laugh, I tried to work out what to do about the fox. One thing seemed clear: something was wrong with this animal. He was either old or injured and was unable to find anything else to eat. If it were winter and food were scarce, a healthy fox might keep coming after my chickens. But it was midsummer, and the fox ought to have plenty of other things to eat.

I don't like to see animals of any kind suffer. But I couldn't afford to keep buying new chickens, and the solution of trapping and relocating the fox was out of the question. Rigging up an electric fence could have worked, but that kind of expense was out of our budget.

So while I was out on my pastoral calls in the village, I paid a visit to Joe, a farmer friend of mine. He had an air rifle with a telescopic sight on it and offered to let me borrow it. I'd learned how to shoot rifles during my police training, so if the fox came back, I'd be ready.

About three in the morning, the chickens began their mad squawking.

I hopped out of bed and peered out the window. Sure enough, the fox was back. I hurried downstairs and made my way into my office, where I'd hidden the rifle out of sight from the girls. I slipped in several pellets and crept into the kitchen. Looking out the window, I saw the fox clearly in the twilight.

The chickens were still squawking madly as I knelt down by the window, opened it carefully and pointed the barrel out of the window towards the fox. Peering through the telescopic sight, I lined him up in the crosshairs.

Just as I was about to squeeze the trigger, Kathy walked into the kitchen.

"Graham darling," she said, "what are you doing?"

"I am just about to shoot him," I told her. "He's in the garden."

"You can't do that, it's not legal."

"Of course it is."

"No it's not. You can't shoot the ..."

I pulled the trigger. The pellet hit the old fox, and he dropped dead.

"I've got him," I said, jumping to my feet. "I've blown him across the fence."

Kathy looked at me, terror-stricken.

A word of marital advice. If a fox kills your chickens, and you get the bright idea to borrow a rifle, it's best to tell your wife ahead of time. At the time, all Kathy knew was this: she'd woken up from a deep sleep to find her husband pointing a gun out the window. I'd been gone all day, and the last thing we'd talked about was my adventure with the milk van. Still half asleep, she was sure I'd assassinated the milkman in the middle of the night for catching me in the next-door neighbour's garden the previous night. Once I'd assured Kathy that I'd shot the fox, not the milkman, I went outside.

The fox lay dead on the other side of the fence. He was ancient; his coat was covered in maggots, and his teeth were overgrown. Killing him had been an act of kindness. We had a tarpaulin in the vicarage, and I brought it out and wrapped the carcass in it. Now what to do with him?

The key thing was to get rid of the body quietly. Blasting foxes from the kitchen window is not the sort of thing that vicars are supposed to go do, so the fewer people who knew, the better. I'd have to tell the neighbours and Joe, but that was as far as I wanted it to go.

Early the next morning, I took the fox and the rifle out to Joe's farm.

"Can you get rid of this for me?" I asked, lifting the fox from the boot. "I don't want anyone to know about it. It's not a proper thing for the vicar to do."

"Sure, Graham," he said, taking the carcass from me. "It'll be our secret."

All this happened on the day we had a parish communion and healing service at St Mary's. Afterwards we all went down to the pub. A roar went up the moment I walked through the doors, as I was greeted by a round of applause.

"Good shot, Vicar," someone called out.

"Way to go, John Wayne," someone else said.

The problem with living in a small village is that there are no secrets. Everyone knew about "John Wayne," the fox-shooting vicar.

I may be wrong, but I believe the church is obsessed with young people. As a priest, I was constantly hearing moans of, "Let's get the young people into church. We've got to have more young people." People believe that if we could draw in the young, the church would grow. But they don't consider that those young people generally grow up, go off to university, get jobs and never come back, so the church never grows.

When I came to St Mary's, my idea was to get the people fifty and over into the church. They're the ones who are more likely to worry about God, because they're going to be facing death a lot sooner than the young ones will.

The first change we made was to have every service be a communion service. I also made it a policy never to turn anyone away from communion. Christians believe that as we share the bread and the wine, God is present and gives us grace. By inviting people to come and have communion, we give them a chance to experience God's love. Over the years, I saw God change people's lives little by little as they came and had communion. If we had turned them away from the communion table, we would have pushed them away from God's love.

In Cloughton, we found that many of the men in the village had never been confirmed, and the Church of England says that people have to be confirmed to participate in communion. Most of the women got confirmed when they were younger, but the men missed out. That meant they were too embarrassed to come to church. And asking a man who's fifty or seventy years old to come to confirmation classes was a nonstarter – those classes are meant for teenagers.

Instead, when new people came to church, I would talk to them and find out what they knew about God. Before and after every service, I'd stand at the door of the church and greet people, which gave me a chance to talk to visitors and make them feel welcome. After a few weeks, I'd say to them, "Why don't you come and have communion?"

We reversed the normal order to make it easier for people to meet God at church, making them part of the congregation and letting them come to communion before confirmation. And when the bishop came round next for confirmation, he confirmed the adults along with the teenagers. When the men in their fifties and sixties were confirmed, they'd start to bring their mates along to church.

We did things to make church enjoyable as well. We'd have golf days, and all the men at church would bring their friends along and have a great time. I was an awful golfer, so they'd enjoy beating the vicar on the golf course.

We wanted people to know that Jesus was a fun guy to be around. Christians have a bad reputation, most of it our own fault. We present ourselves as the church of the boring old gits. We don't laugh, we don't joke, we don't enjoy ourselves, and we're seen as being miserable, telling people, "You mustn't do this" and "You mustn't do that." But my picture of Jesus is of a man who loved to laugh and share time with others. That's one reason I begin every sermon with a joke, to put people at ease and to let them know that God enjoys it when we laugh.

Before long, we had a fifty-fifty split of men and women in the church, which is quite rare since many congregations end up as holy clubs for women, with men few and far between. The more men showed up in church, the more it became natural for the women in the congregation to bring their husbands. First the older women brought their husbands, and then the younger women brought their husbands and children along.

When I arrived at St Mary's in 1999, the church had fifteen members. Within three years, we ended up with ninety regular members and thirty-five children in the youth section. That's not bad growth in a village of 292 people. At one point, we realised that our attendance was something like five or six times the national average.

Beneath all of the activity was a great deal of prayer. Every morning at eight o'clock, Ros, the reader at St Mary's, and I would go into the church and pray. We'd meet with a few other faithful prayers and together bring the needs of the parish and the world before God. Everything started and ended in prayer. We'd ask God to send people to the church, and we would pray for opportunities to speak with people about God. God built a very strong church in Cloughton during those years.

12

SHADOWMANCER

Early one Saturday morning in October 2002, a lorry pulled
in the driveway and parked outside the vicarage. The driver,
a short man wearing a blue work jacket and work boots, hopped
down from the truck and rapped on the front door.

"Delivery of books for G. P. Taylor," he said in a voice far too
loud for that time of the morning.

"That's me," I said, opening the door.

"Right, where's your warehouse?"

"I haven't got a warehouse."

"You haven't got a warehouse? I've twenty-five hundred
books here for you. What are you going to do with them?"

"I'll put them in the house," I said.

He paused for a moment and gave me an odd stare. "All
right," he said, looking around. "Where's your forklift?"

"I haven't got a forklift."

"What do you have then?" he asked, exasperated.

"I've got a wife and three kids."

"You'd better get them out here," he said. "I haven't got all
morning." With that, he turned and walked back to the truck
while I went inside to get the girls and Kathy. By the time we
all were outside, the driver had opened the back of the lorry
to reveal the biggest stack of books I had ever seen, all shrink-
wrapped together on a wooden pallet.

The driver cut away the plastic and began tossing the books down in bundles of ten. Twenty-five hundred books is a lot – it's like ten typical bookcases standing back to back. What to do with all these books wasn't something I had considered when I ordered them from the printer six weeks earlier.

The first order of business was getting them off the lorry. Everyone pitched in, even Lydia, who was only two. The driver was still shaking his head as he closed up the lorry, muttering something about "no forklift" as he walked back to the cab and drove off.

We put books in every spare corner we could find – in my office, under the beds, in the loo. In the hallway, we stacked them six feet high, leaving a narrow pathway in the middle. When we were done, I opened up one of the packets to get a closer look. In the top corner, a bright moon hung in a clear night sky, its rays lighting up the sea beneath it. The word *Shadowmancer* was laid out in black letters outlined with red, with the name G. P. Taylor underneath.

While I stood admiring the cover, Kathy surveyed our house. A look of horror covered her face when she returned. "You've got to get rid of these" was all she said before going to make herself a cup of tea.

I'm going to be stuck with these books for the rest of my life, I thought to myself.

Almost two years earlier, I'd been at home in the vicarage, reading a copy of *The Amber Spyglass* by Philip Pullman. I'd heard a great deal about the book. Newspapers and literary critics praised it. Christian groups wanted to burn it. I wanted to know what all the commotion was about.

Fifty pages into this award-winning, bestselling book for children twelve and up, here's what I'd learned: God is a liar.

God is senile. God is the enemy of humanity. I started to get mad.

Pullman's book reworks Milton's *Paradise Lost* so that Satan's side are the heroes. Early on in the book, two rebel angels spill God's great "secret": "The Authority, God the Creator, the Lord, Yahweh, El, Adonai, the King, the Father, the Almighty – those were the names he gave himself. He was never the creator. He was an angel like ourselves – the first angel, true, the most powerful angel, but he was formed of Dust as we are.... He told all who came after him that he had created them, but it was a lie."

That's just the beginning. Later the Authority is revealed as a senile, decrepit creature, the figurehead leader of Pullman's Kingdom of Heaven. Pullman describes the Authority this way: "He was so old, and he was terrified, crying like a baby and cowering." And, "The old one was uttering a wordless groaning whimper that went on and on, and grinding his teeth, and compulsively plucking at himself with his free hand."

I became so angry while reading *The Amber Spyglass* that I had to put it down. What does it do to a child, I wondered, to be told that God is a senile, decrepit old man who would be better off dead.

As dangerous theologically as I thought Pullman's book was, I believed he had every right to publish it. I don't want to live in a country where books are burned, where authors are not free to write what matters most to them. But the disturbing thoughts about the effects of such a bestseller kept running through my mind that night, and for many nights afterwards.

My fears were being realised. During the summer of 2000, the Pagan Federation in the United Kingdom announced that they had hired a youth officer to deal with all the enquiries they were getting from teenagers who wanted to become witches. The federation was "swamped" with calls, the federation's media officer, Andy Norfolk, told the BBC. The reason Norfolk gave was the overwhelming popularity of television shows like *Buffy the Vampire Slayer* and *Sabrina the Teenage Witch* and the Harry Potter books. He also said that the Christian church had failed to offer spirituality that appealed to teenagers, and pagans were now filling the gap because they offered "direct communication with the divine."

The frightening part was that Norfolk was partly right. We in the church *were* failing these teenagers. They were looking for some sign of a God who was interested in their lives, who cared for them. Since they couldn't see that kind of God in church – in all likelihood because they'd never been there – these kids turned to the Pagan Federation instead. I'd been down that road thirty years earlier and wanted to shout out to these kids that that wasn't the way and that God loved them tenderly.

From looking at the children's bestseller lists, I could see that kids wanted to read about the supernatural. Books with supernatural themes – Harry Potter, Darren Shan's vampire stories, *The Amber Spyglass*, to name a few – sell in the millions. Most of them deal with questions of good and evil, death and immortality. If kids couldn't find God in church, then they certainly could find spiritual answers on the children's shelves of their nearest bookshop. But aside from C. S. Lewis's *Chronicles of Narnia* and J. R. R. Tolkien's *The Lord of the Rings*, both written in the 1950s, few books or films for children show a positive view of God.

Instead of trying to ban Pullman's *His Dark Materials* or Rowling's Harry Potter, Christians need to learn from them, just like those authors learned from C. S. Lewis and J. R. R. Tolkien. If people won't come to church to find God, we've got to bring God and spiritual truth out to the people. People may no longer be religious, but they are spiritual, and the desire to satisfy that part of our nature will go on forever. There will always be an audience for epic tales of the battle between good and evil, and I believe the church has got to tell them.

Over the next few months, my worries about children's books, films and television continued to mount. Hannah and Abigail were becoming teenagers, and what would the church offer them in the place of Buffy, Lyra and Will? Book burnings or banning? Someone had to offer an alternative.

All that was running through my mind on 21 March 2002 when I went to speak at St John Newland church in Hull, about forty miles south of Cloughton. Because of my background in the occult and witchcraft, from time to time, churches have invited me to lecture on that subject. That night, all I could talk about was children's books. I told the congregation that instead of being angry or fearful, we needed to do something positive. Someone needed to write books that meet our desire for a good story and show a God who is involved in the lives of people. I hoped someone in the audience might take me up on the idea.

At the end of the service, I stood in the back, greeting people. Most thanked me for the sermon, but no one seemed inspired to go out and write the next children's bestseller. Then I saw a woman near the end of the queue with an intense look on her face. *Now I've done it*, I thought, and braced for what I thought would be an angry comment.

She came up to me and looked me straight in my eyes. "If you think you can do a better job," she said, "why don't you write a children's book where God wins?" With that, off she went.

Her words stuck with me as I walked out to my car. I wondered, *Could I write a book? What would it be about?* As I headed north towards Cloughton, I turned the idea over and over in my head. I was no writer; the longest thing I'd written since leaving theological college was a page-and-a-half sermon each week. But I supposed it couldn't hurt to try.

The sky had been overcast when I left Hull, and a storm broke out just as I started over the moors. The further north I drove, the blacker the sky became. Then the clouds burst, and rain came down in sheets. The pouring rain swallowed the light from the headlamps of my Vauxhall Cavalier, so that I could barely see beyond the edge of the car's bonnet as I moved along the moor. Lightning split the sky as thunderclaps resounded overheard. Everything felt black and horrible.

I could see the lighthouse at Flamborough shining away in the blackness, about twenty miles off. All of a sudden an idea for a story began forming in my mind – it felt like I was downloading it from somewhere. I began seeing smugglers out on the sea on a stormy night and a figure dressed in black with a wizard's staff held high in his hand, urging the storm on. A stranger was onboard the ship, a boy from Africa who was filled with God's power. He had with him what looked like one of the angels from the Ark of the Covenant in the Old Testament. Some lines from the Gospel of John popped into my head as well, about the light coming into the world and the darkness not being able to put it out.

The next morning, I started writing the story down.

"It was a still October night." With those six words, my career as a writer was launched. But an hour later, with the waves crashing over the decks of the *Friendship*, a collier brig carrying one of the main characters to England, my career was already on the rocks. For the third time, the ancient computer on my desk had crashed. As the machine hummed, blipped and came slowly back to life, I considered again how foolish the idea of writing a book was. I knew nothing about writing fiction. I felt like I was setting off on a journey with no idea of my destination or how long it would take to get there.

On the other hand, I had nothing better to do that morning. The weather was still too cold for my weekly game of golf.

Besides, my hip ached every time I walked more than a quarter mile or so. It was the only injury from the beating in Pickering that remained with me. So when the computer came back to life, I set my word processor to save every two minutes. That way, when the computer crashed again, I wouldn't lose too much. That done, I began typing away.

The first character to show up was Obadiah Demurral, vicar of Ravenscar. I was inspired by the extraordinary characters from the eighteenth-century history I'd been reading. Priests from that period would dress in clerical black from head to foot, with white shirts and collar ties. I pictured Obadiah as a tall, thin man with long grey hair and a very rugged, handsome appearance. He was someone who looked holy on the outside but was corrupted on the inside by money and power. When ministers, who are supposed to serve God, get too successful – their church grows too big, or they become a bishop, or they end up preaching on television – they can run into trouble. Like Obadiah, they start out with good intentions, but somewhere along the line, things go terribly wrong.

As a vicar in the eighteenth century, Obadiah would have had access to a great deal of rent. The locals would pay tithes and rents to the church, and he could make himself rich by pilfering the collection box. But he wanted more. He wanted power enough to force God to do his bidding. To do that, Obadiah had to get hold of the Ark of the Covenant, which had peculiar supernatural powers in the Old Testament. That became the driving force of the story. Demurral steals part of the Ark of the Covenant and brings it to England, in hopes of using it against God.

A lot of people today treat God as if he's a wimp, but that's not what we see in the Bible. God is the creator of the universe, and he's not somebody to be blasphemed against or treated lightly. I wanted to give some muscle back to God, so I had the idea that the cherubim – statues of angels that adorned the

Ark – had been stolen from Ethiopia, where the Ark had been hidden. I changed the name from *cherubim* – which conjures up images of baby-faced angels with wings – to *Keruvim*. The word was a transliteration of the Hebrew for *angel*. Old Testament angels are huge, eight-foot tall creatures with swords who fight for God. That kind of angel would be sure to get a kid's attention.

Because I didn't want the book to be completely dark and serious, Obadiah needed a sidekick, someone to give comic relief. There'd been a civics lecture in the village earlier in the year, and a town crier had come to talk. He was a little, round, fat guy with wispy hair and said that the town criers were always named Beadle. He popped in my mind when I was looking for a character to pair with Obadiah. Whereas Obadiah was in control of things and was powerful and self-assured, Beadle was in his shadow and was always messing things up.

From that first morning in March, the story took shape little by little each day. Most days I found ten or fifteen minutes to write. The odd thing was, once I put the characters on the page, they took on lives of their own. They started to act and behave in ways that I did not completely control. As soon as they opened their mouths, their words would change the course of the story. The process was very exciting as the characters started to talk to each other and things started to develop. I never knew from one day to the next where the story was going.

I was a novice and needed help with the mechanics of writing a novel. As I approached the dozens of Harry Potter books stacked up at Ottakar's bookstore, I tried to be inconspicuous as I picked one up and started counting. One hundred. Two hundred. Three hundred. Four hundred and sixty-eight words on a page. Next I counted the number of pages in each chapter;

about ten each. I pulled out a ruler and measured the margin; it was about half an inch. I noticed the paragraphs were all short, not more than a few inches long.

That's all I wanted to know. If it was good enough for J. K. Rowling, it was good enough for me. Her example inspired me. After all, when she started out, she was just a single mum writing in cafés while her daughter slept in the pram. If she could write a book, why couldn't I?

When I got home, I set the margins on my computer screen so that it would have 468 words on the page. I made my chapters about the same length as in the Harry Potter book. I thought, *This must be how you write a book*. And while I was writing, I made sure the paragraphs were always about an inch or two long.

One by one, more characters began to appear in the book. First came Raphah, a boy from Ethiopia, looking for the stolen Keruvim. The Ethiopian Orthodox Church claims to have the Ark of the Covenant hidden away, so it made sense to have Raphah come from Africa. His name comes from the Hebrew word for *healer*, and he was a total opposite of Obadiah Demurral. Raphah believes in Riathamus, the God that Obadiah has rejected. When C. S. Lewis wanted to put a Jesus-like figure in his stories, he made him a lion and called him Aslan. So I did the same thing. There's an old English word, *riathamus*, that was used for King Arthur, and it means "king of the kings." That's what God is, the King of the Kings, so the name fit.

Having a black hero also appealed to me since there are few black heroes in children's books. Harry Potter is a white, Anglo-Saxon Protestant with a scar on his face. Lyra, the heroine of Philip Pullman's *Dark Materials*, is a lovely, little, white virgin girl. So having a hero come from Africa would be new and interesting. Plus it made for great contrast. Raphah lands in civilized England and finds it a savage place. He's the outsider, from a "less enlightened land," but he's the most civilized character in the book.

Along the way, I was trying to say something about Jesus as well. We've got two different versions of Jesus, the one in the Bible and the one in the church. St Mary's Cloughton has a stained glass window of a white, Anglo-Saxon, six-foot tall, blonde, blue-eyed, Protestant Jesus. But Jesus was actually probably five feet nine or ten and dark skinned and would have fit nicely as a refugee getting off a boat. And he would have faced the same religious intolerance and persecution that many such people are facing today. He was the black guy from the north of the country who didn't fit in. He was the outcast who came with radical ideas.

Thomas followed soon on Raphah's heels. Like many of the heroes in children's books, Thomas was an orphan. Parents can be cumbersome in a children's book, for they are always saying what not to do. But getting rid of the parents gives the ultimate freedom. And Thomas needed a friend, so Kate appeared. If the book was going to have a girl main character, she was going to have some meat on her. In the first scene between Kate and Thomas, she beats him up and then pulls a gun on him. Her father is the sheriff, but he's been a drunk since Kate's mother died, so she's on her own.

The last character to show up was Jacob Crane. For centuries, smugglers made Scarborough their home, so Jacob's a smuggler. He's rough around the edges and does things his way. He's not going to be taken in by anyone. Of all the characters, Jacob Crane is the most like me. He's had a bit of a history, but at some point, he's realised that there's more to life than what he knows. He is looking to find out more about God but doesn't want to give up being tough and independent.

A year after beginning *Shadowmancer*, the adventure was drawing to a close. Every day, sometimes only for ten minutes, I'd gone away into this enchanted world, loving every second. The story had taken on a life of its own and was unfolding on the computer screen before my very eyes. For two hundred pages, Thomas, Kate and Raphah had raced over the moors, through smugglers' caves and wild forests, with Demurral or his demonic henchmen at their heels. Now they were trapped in Whitby, with St Mary's as their last hope of refuge. I wondered how it all would end.

After a few hours more in that enchanted world, the ending came to me. A few pages after a climactic showdown at St Mary's, the characters said goodbye to one another, and I typed those famous last words, "The End." Then I hit the save button and listened as the computer hummed to life, putting the story under lock and key. I loaded some paper in my printer, and an hour or so later, I had a pile of about 250 pages. My first book was finished.

That night, after the girls were in bed, I brought the stack of pages to Kathy in the front room.

"Here," I said. "Why don't you take a look at this?"

"What is it?"

"My book."

"It's finished?"

"It's all there."

Kathy was the first person to read *Shadowmancer*. I wanted to have the whole thing written before anyone saw it. Over the next few days, I tried to wait patiently for her to finish it and prayed more than a few times that she'd like it. When she finally turned over the last page, she smiled at me.

"It's amazing," she said.

"You like it?"

"I do," she said. "It's astounding, Graham. I didn't know you could write like this."

If Kathy hadn't liked the book, if she hadn't believed in me, *Shadowmancer* might have died right there. But she did like it, and that gave me the confidence to let other people read it and to dream of actually publishing it.

Next to read it was Mary Evans, a great friend from St Mary's Cloughton. Mary edits medical journals and books and in her youth worked for the poet T. S. Elliot. She's also the most forthright person I know, and I thought she'd give me an honest appraisal of the book without sparing my feelings. She liked *Shadowmancer* too.

"I don't think you're going to get it published," she told me. She told me how the children's book market is very competitive, and despite the success of Harry Potter, the chances of an unknown author getting published were slim. She encouraged me to try but told me not to get my hopes too high. "There are too many other books to vie against," she told me.

The online editing consultant I sent *Shadowmancer* to was less kind. I found them while searching the Internet and emailed them a copy of the book. For a fee, they promised to critique the book. Their response came by snail mail a few weeks later. The gist of the letter was that *Shadowmancer* was written in Victorian language, and as a historical thriller, it had no commercial future. Some writers keep their rejection letters and pin them to the wall as motivation to keep writing. But I binned it and moped around for a week, feeling sorry for myself.

But then I decided to follow up on a conversation I'd had with Mary about self-publishing. Since I couldn't get the book published through the trade, I'd find another way.

The Yamaha roared to life as I kicked the starter and turned the throttle. A smile spread on my face as I rode through the centre of Cloughton and up to the top of the moor. The wind screamed in my face as the speedometer reached 90 miles per hour on a flat stretch of road. As a dip approached, I slowed and banked the motorcycle into a turn, then accelerated up another hill.

The events of the past months raced through my mind. My phone call to Mary Evans led me to the Society of Authors, who sent me a pamphlet on self-publishing and a list of book printers. Another friend owned a printing company and lent me a computer with Quark, a design programme, on it, so the book could be typeset. Three friends volunteered to edit the book: Sally Maynard and Caroline from church read some of the chapters and gave me some advice on how to tighten the story up, while Mary Evans read through the book for me, searching for typos, all for a couple of bottles of wine. Percy Hope, an artist from Burniston, offered to design the cover for free. To avoid any confusion with Graham Taylor the football coach, we listed the author's name as G. P. Taylor on the book cover.

The book was finally ready to go to the printer; only one last detail remained. I pulled over to the side of the road, checked both ways and turned the Yahama towards Cloughton.

A printer in Finland had offered the best price: £3,500 for 2,500 copies of a 252-page book with a four-colour paperback cover. Shadowmancer had been 268 pages long, but the extra 16 pages would have cost a few hundred extra pounds. So I have to admit that the book ends rather abruptly. Kathy lent me £400 from her savings, and the rest would have to come from selling my motorcycle.

I like to tell people that the reason I self-published Shadowmancer was because no publisher would take it. That's only partly true. The rest of the story is that I was afraid. I was a fat, middle-aged, boring vicar who thought his best years had passed him by. My lot in life, I was sure, was to remain a vicar in a small village until I was too old to carry on. I was going to be a foot soldier for God, someone who will do the grunt work of the church without much recognition. Still, something inside of me dreamt of doing something amazing with my life. If that was going to happen, then the Yamaha – no matter how much I loved it – had to go.

After my last ride, I drove to the motorcycle shop and parked the bike outside. They offered me £3,000, enough to pay the final printer's bill. I took the money, handed over the keys and walked out of the shop, never looking back.

13

HOTTER THAN POTTER

The weather outside was miserable. The temperature was hovering right above freezing, and a driving rain made it a perfect day for staying home and curling up by a fire. But that was not to be. Kathy and I drove north towards Whitby with several boxes of *Shadowmancer* in the boot. Maddy, the owner of the Whitby bookshop, had graciously offered to host my first book signing. Since the book was set in and around Whitby, and given that I'd spent five years as a priest there, she thought the event would draw a crowd. She also was the first person ever to buy a copy of *Shadowmancer*.

The rain worsened the closer we got to Whitby. Earlier I'd hoped that perhaps a hundred people would show up. But with this weather, we'd be lucky if twenty were there.

We parked on a hilly street near the centre of town. I grabbed the boxes from the boot while Kathy sheltered us from the rain as best she could. As we got closer to the bookshop, we were heartened to see a queue outside the shop, winding past the White Horse and Griffin Hotel and down Church Street.

Maddy, the shop owner, met us at the door and guided us through the crowded bookstore to the children's section. A table and chair were already prepared for the signing.

Well, this is it, I thought.

"Are you ready?" she asked.

"I think so."

"All right then," she said, and called the crowd to attention.

We sold two hundred books that day. I signed copies and chatted with many of my old friends who had turned up to wish me well. It was fantastic.

"We'll have to do this again for your next book," Maddy said several hours later as the last customer left.

"Let me sell a few more of this one before I think about another book," I said. "I've still got a lot more back at home." We had a laugh, and then Kathy and I walked back to the car, hand in hand.

The book seemed to take on a life of its own; the success at the Whitby bookshop led to more invitations for book signings. Waterstone's in Scarborough was next, where we sold another hundred books. I thought I'd have to use all my old record-plugger's tricks to sell my book, but people were calling me instead.

Hosting a book signing didn't involve much risk for bookshops. All the books were on sale, with return conditions – so if people bought them, the shop made money, and if no one bought them, I took the copies home. All it cost the shops was their time.

When I first decided to self-publish *Shadowmancer*, the audience I had in mind was friends, family and people in the surrounding villages. I'd never considered that people outside the area might be interested. But the local bookshops were overwhelmed by their customers' response to *Shadowmancer*, and they started to spread the word to other shops or to their head office. Since people could only get the book from me, they began ringing the vicarage at all hours.

The *Scarborough News* got wind of the book's popularity and wrote a story about this vicar who'd written a book like the Harry Potter books and sold his motorcycle to publish it. So people would call, looking to buy a copy because they'd seen it in the paper. A friend of mine set up a *Shadowmancer* website so people could place orders. We'd collect orders during the week and have book-packing day on Friday, my day off. The first one was calm, as we only had about fifty books to post.

I was learning some hard lessons about the book business. *Shadowmancer* had a cover price of £5.99, but all of that money didn't go to me. Bookshops pay a discounted rate for their books, and in the case of *Shadowmancer*, that was £2.30. The books had cost £1.25 each to print, so that left a profit, after printing cost, of £1. That worked fine if I sold them in a local bookshop. But what I hadn't realised was that if I sold them to someone out of town, I would end up paying about a pound a copy to post the books. I'd also forgotten to include the cost of gaffer paper, cello-tape, envelopes and all the other supplies. When all those costs were added up, I was actually paying people to buy my book.

The second week was frantic. We had three hundred books to be posted. We'd saved up orders all week and spent a good portion of the day packing and labelling them. That week, I spent £234 in postage and £35 in cello-tape alone. Unfortunately, not much money was coming in from the books. Bookshops work on sixty-day credit, so we had all these expenses, and no money was coming in. I could see Christmas approaching and my bank balance going down rapidly.

After the second week, I took out a map and began marking all the places where we'd posted books. Some had gone to York, to Nottingham, to London, to Scotland, to Wales – it was like a rash spreading across the country in little clusters. I couldn't understand how all this was happening. So whenever someone called looking for a copy of *Shadowmancer*, I'd ask them how they'd heard about the book. The story was almost always the same. Someone would find the book in a shop and read it. They'd like it, so they'd ring a family member or a friend and say, "Hey, I found this really good book. It's called *Shadowmancer*. You can only buy it by getting it off the vicar." Before long, I'd get a call or an email saying, "Are you the fat vicar who writes books? If you are, I'd like to get a copy of *Shadowmancer*."

The third week was absolute madness. We had 1,700 books to post, most of them going to Waterstone's. The head office had heard about the book and offered to take 1,500. Suzan, our next-door neighbour, came over to help pack them, as Kathy and I couldn't handle it by ourselves. We started at 8:00 a.m. and wrapped, taped and labelled books all day. From the first day she'd seen the book, Suzan had a prophetic insight that it was going to be "a big success," therefore she wanted to lend a hand. By midafternoon, we were clearing out all the hiding places where books were stuffed. The hallway was emptied, then the loo, my office, out from under our beds and the kid's beds. At the end of the day, the books all ended in a massive stack in the middle of the front room.

I made four or five trips to the post office the next morning, ferrying the books in shifts. Eventually, even the post-office staff members were getting tired of seeing me.

"Not more books," one of them said as I walked in at the end of my first trip. "Where are we supposed to put them all? What's going on here?" The post office was small and not set up for the massive order I was bringing in.

"This is the last of them," I said, heaving a pile of books onto the counter, dreading what the total for posting would be this time.

The fourth book-packing Friday was quiet. We had only a few copies of *Shadowmancer* left and had been telling anyone who called that they could get the book at Waterstone's. After lunch, I posted a few copies and came home, anticipating an afternoon of doing absolutely nothing. It had been almost four weeks since my last day off, and I needed a rest.

I prayed that God would somehow intervene and take this newfound burden away. Little did I know that he had already done just that.

A week later, I got a phone call from a literary agent, Caroline Sheldon, who asked if I'd come to her London office in Notting Hill for a meeting. She thought *Shadowmancer* was a "hot book" and was sure she could find a publisher for it. I agreed to see her, bringing along the few copies I had left. Over tea, she asked if I had a publisher in mind. Faber and Faber came to mind – as a teenager, I'd sent them some poems – so she pitched the book to them. Faber asked for additional copies for their staff to read over the Christmas holidays. When the holidays were over, we had a deal, and I had my first advance: £7,500. Not exactly J. K. Rowling money, but it was more than half of my annual salary.

Faber originally planned to publish *Shadowmancer* in the autumn. But soon after we signed a publishing deal, news of the book reached the national newspapers. In February, the *Telegraph* ran a story about *Shadowmancer*, with the headline: "A Magical Tale of Vicars and Witches." The article played up how Harry Potter had inspired *Shadowmancer* and how I'd sold my motorcycle to self-publish it. Soon other national stories followed. By the end of the month, I was on *Richard and Judy* – a British daytime TV show as popular as *Oprah* in America.

I came down to London by GNER train on a bitterly cold February day and was met at King's Cross station by a limousine. I was whisked into the back of this limo and sent off with a press assistant to do the show at the ITV television studios.

At the studio, I felt like I'd fallen into another world. Champagne and chocolate were waiting for me in the green room (a lounge where guests on a television show wait before going on air). I gave the bottle of champagne to the production assistant, as I didn't drink alcohol at that point in my life, and had a wonderful time chatting to her while waiting for the show.

Being on television is very odd. You sit on a couch and have a lovely chat with one or two people as if you were sitting on your couch at home having a cup of tea with them. You've no idea if ten million people are watching the show or only ten.

After five minutes, the interview was over. I shook hands with Richard and Judy, and the production assistant escorted me from the set. From there, it was back to the green room and then on to the limo.

The driver dropped me off at King's Cross, or "Hooker City," as the local police call it. Many Americans, having read about King's Cross in the Harry Potter books, go there as tourists and are amazed to find out it's in an area where prostitution is common. I went from *Richard and Judy* to Hooker City all in the space of about fifteen minutes, so it really did bring me back down to earth.

Faber paid for my train ticket, but I was still a small-time author, so there was no first-class ticket for me. After my five minutes of fame, I was shipped back to the north of England in the coach class with all the Friday-night drunks. When we arrived in York, the train to Scarborough had been cancelled, and I had to share a taxi with about five other guys to get home.

So much for the life of a famous author. *I bet this never happens to Philip Pullman,* I thought on the taxi ride home.

When launching *Shadowmancer*, Faber decided to take advantage of all the press around the release of J. K. Rowling's next book. After they learned that *Harry Potter and the Order of the Phoenix* was due out on 21 June 2003, they scheduled *Shadowmancer* to be released the same day. The book got a boost in publicity when Ottakar's chose it as children's book of the month for June, over Harry Potter.

Since *Shadowmancer* had done so well as a self-published book, Faber did very little editing and could publish it quickly. The major change was a flashy new cover, featuring the ruins of the Whitby Abbey. For the first time, I also had to write an author bio for the book cover. The first draft went something like this: "G. P. Taylor is a fat, boring, forty-three-year-old priest who has a lively, growing Anglican church in North Yorkshire." But who's going to buy a book by that guy? I didn't want to scare off all the people I wanted to read *Shadowmancer* – those who didn't consider themselves Christians or didn't know God. So scratching that draft out, I finally came up with this: "Graham Taylor has spent the whole of his life searching for the hidden secrets of the universe. He lectures on the paranormal and folklore and lives in a secluded graveyard."

Every word was true. I've searched for the secrets of the universe all my life, and we lived in the middle of a church graveyard. I just wasn't going to shout out "I'm a vicar" and have people not buy the book because of that.

On Friday, 28 June, six days after *Shadowmancer* was released, I set off from the vicarage at five in the morning for a day of book signings and press events in London. I drove in my old car, praying the whole way that it wouldn't break down. The book was already selling briskly, and by the end of the first month, it would be number one on the bestseller paperback lists.

I arrived at the Faber offices around nine o'clock, and from there was whisked from one event to another. The bookstores were packed with kids who wanted me to sign their books and have their photographs taken with me. In between signings, I met with reporters and recounted the whole story: about selling my motorcycle and self-publishing the book and how I didn't hate Harry Potter or think he was evil but wanted to show kids a different way to look at the world. The signings and interviews came so fast that they are blurred together in my mind. It was great fun, and the whole time, I kept wondering when I was going to wake up and find out it was all a dream.

Once all the events were done, it was on to a Faber summer party, where my editors and Caroline toasted the success of *Shadowmancer* and wished me well. Around 8:00 p.m., I said my goodbyes and made my way back to the car. With any luck, I'd be home by midnight. Faber offered to put me up in a hotel for the night, but I dreaded the idea of facing the traffic in London again, even on a Saturday. More important, I'd missed too many mornings with the girls because of my work in the past and wanted to get home to them.

The M1 was a nightmare. Traffic crawled along leaving London, which was to be expected, but I was sure that things would clear up north of the city. But after a few hours of driving, I saw the dreadful signs of road resurfacing. Several lanes were shut down, and traffic had slowed to ten miles per hour. This went on for hours and hours, and I wasn't able to get off the motorway.

Somewhere between Nottingham and Yorkshire, I developed a throbbing pain in the back of my leg. I tried stretching it out, thinking it was a cramp, but that didn't help. Rubbing it with my free hand was no good either. Something was wrong with my breathing as well. I felt like I'd been running up a flight of steps and was short of breath.

I concentrated, trying to breathe in deeply and slowly, but it was no good; I couldn't catch my breath. A smarter or less stubborn person might have pulled off the road. But I felt that if I could just get back home, I'd be okay, as if being with Kathy and the kids would make me well again.

I gripped the steering wheel tightly, willing myself to keep going. Finally, I caught sight of the turnoff for York. The traffic backup eased as soon as I pulled onto the road leading to York. From there, I drove almost by instinct past the city, then into Scarborough and north to Cloughton.

It was two in the morning when I finally pulled down the long, gravel drive leading to the vicarage. I heaved a sigh of relief, prizing my finger off of the steering wheel. My leg throbbed in pain and my breath was still short, but I was home.

Getting upstairs was painful, but within five minutes, I was in the bathroom, gobbling down aspirin for my leg. After peeking in on each of the girls, I climbed into bed. The familiar touch of the sheets and duvet eased my wearied body. I settled in for what I hoped would be a long, restful sleep.

Kathy rolled over and smiled as I lay down beside her. A minute later, we were both asleep.

The pain in my chest was nearly unbearable. I jerked up, wide awake. My heart was pounding, doing two hundred beats a minute. It felt like Keith Moon, the maniacal drummer of the Who, was playing the drums in the centre of my chest. The clock by the bed stand read 2:30. I'd been asleep for less than half an hour.

"What is it, Graham?" Kathy asked in a startled voice.

I choked out, "My chest, my heart is pounding. I can't breathe."

Kathy turned on the light, looking at me with concern. I was pale, shaking with pain and sweat pouring down my face. Her nurse's training took over.

"Graham, you need to be in hospital," she said. "I'll call an ambulance."

"There's no need," I protested, grabbing hold of her arm. "I'll be all right. I just need to rest."

"If something's wrong with your heart, you need to be seen right away. I'm calling an ambulance." She started for the door.

With all my strength, I stood up. "Don't call an ambulance. I'll drive myself."

The hospital in Scarborough was fifteen minutes away, and it would take the ambulance at least twenty minutes to scramble and get here, then another fifteen minute ride back.

"I could be there in half the time," I told Kathy. She would have driven me herself, but didn't want to rush out in the middle of the night and terrify the girls.

She hesitated. "Graham, that's not a good idea. I'll call an ambulance."

"I'll drive myself," I told Kathy. "Really. It'll be all right."

I didn't dare admit it to Kathy, but I knew something was dreadfully wrong. I was barely admitting it to myself, instead thinking of a line from one of my favourite movies as a kid, the old American western called *They Died with Their Boots On*. Errol Flynn played General Custer, and when they were surrounded at Little Big Horn, he said, "Keep standing. If you stand up, you'll never die."

I walked carefully down the stairs, those words from General Custer echoing in my mind. "Keep standing, and you won't die." I was still standing; I was still breathing. I was in a lot of pain, but I knew I could make it to the hospital.

The walk to the car was halting. Step, step, gasp for breath. Step, step, gasp for breath. Act normal, and this pain in my chest won't kill me. But when I got to the hospital, it was clear the staff weren't fooled by my routine. As soon as they saw me walk in, gasping for breath, they rushed me to a bed.

"No, no," I told them. "I don't want to lie down, I will be fine." I do not make a good patient.

But the nurse looked me straight in the eye. "You need to lie down, now."

She spoke with such authority that I did what I was told. She began wiring me to a host of machines. Somewhere in the background, I heard the emergency doctor on the phone, calling a consultant.

"Can you get down here right away? We've got a very sick man; he's very poorly."

I started looking around the room, wondering, *Where's the poor bloke who is really sick?* But no one else was in the emergency admissions area, so I soon realised that she was talking about me. Gazing about, I saw a crash trolley right next to me. This was not good.

I am not that sick. That cannot be me she's talking about.

But my whole body was shaking as I lay in bed, my heart pounding away, so I was clearly not well. That was obvious to everyone but me. But vicars don't get much practice being sick. We spend a lot of time in hospitals but are always there for someone else. Then when we are sick, there's no one to call.

Already my mind was racing ahead to Sunday services. It had been nearly three years since I'd taken a Sunday off. It was difficult to find someone to take over five services in one weekend under normal conditions. On such short notice, it would be nearly impossible. I figured I'd have to get better by Sunday morning.

While several nurses and doctors looked me over, another nurse – a friend of mine from school – asked me where Kathy was.

"She's not here."

"All right," she said. "Who brought you?"

"No one. I brought myself."

"You did what?!"

"I drove myself."

She shook her head. "Graham," she said, "You're an idiot."

A few minutes later, the consultant came by and began asking questions. When did my heart start racing? Had this happened before? Was the pain in my leg still there? Had I taken any medication? He told me they suspected that I'd had a deep-vein thrombosis – a blot clot – which had made its way to my heart and set it off. My condition was serious, and it was vital that they slow down my heart.

"Mr Taylor," he said, "we're going to give you some medication for the pain and to try to slow down your heart."

After he left, I started to pray. It was just one word – "Jesus" – over and over again. "Jesus. Jesus. Jesus." At a dire time like this, there was nothing else I could pray. Kathy's face and the faces of Hannah, Abigail and Lydia appeared in my mind. I couldn't bear the thought of leaving them. All of a sudden, the weight of it all crashed down in me. I was going to die, and there was nothing I could do about.

By about six in the morning, the medication began to take effect and my heart began slowing. The pain subsided, and I was able to breathe easier. But my heart wouldn't settle into a normal rhythm; it remained dangerously erratic.

The consultant told me that he wanted to do a treatment in which he would stop my heart with an electric shock. A second shock would restart it. He'd give the medication another hour, until seven o'clock, and then try the treatment.

As soon as the consultant left, I started to talk to God. Having my heart stopped terrified me. I had a dread that if the doctor stopped my heart, I was not going to come out of this alive. "Jesus," I said, "you've got to heal me. You've got to do it now, or this doctor is going to kill me."

Nothing happened. I started bargaining with God, pleading for my life. "Look, God, I'll work even harder at church. I'll do whatever you want. Just don't let me die."

From my bed, I could see the clock on the wall. It read 6:15. I kept pleading with God for the next several minutes, glancing up every few minutes to check the time. At 6:55, the consultant came back in and took my blood pressure and checked my pulse. It was still widely erratic.

"I'll be back at seven o'clock, and we'll do the treatment then."

The clock on the wall read 6:59.

"Look, Jesus," I said, "you are going to have to do it right now. You are going to have to fix my heart right now."

Nothing.

Right, I thought. *I'm just going to have to take matters into my own hands.* I summoned up all my strength. Commandeering some words of Scripture and using my best vicar's voice, I said, "In the name of Jesus, I command this sickness to leave my body."

As soon as the words left my mouth, I felt a horrendous lurching in my chest. For two or three seconds, the monitor let out the long, piercing tone of a flatline. My heart had stopped.

I'm dead. I'm dead. This is it.

Then came another lurch, just as sudden as the first one. I felt my heart beating normally and heard a normal, steady beat on the monitor.

The doctor came hurrying in, wheeling all of the equipment for the procedure. Looking at the monitor, he said, "How strange."

"What's strange?"

"Your heart's beating normally."

"Yeah," I said. "I just asked Jesus to heal me."

The doctor looked at me as if I was mad and ordered a series of tests, all of which came back normal. He sent me home in the middle of the afternoon with strict orders to take at least a fortnight off from work.

Kathy picked me up from the hospital and took me home. I followed the doctor's orders to the letter. Well, at least for one afternoon. When I got home, I went straight to bed. The next morning, I got up early and went back to work.

One reason I went to work was that I was a workaholic. I used to believe in "justification by perspiration" – that if I worked hard enough for God, I would somehow be worthy of his love. That's terrible theology, but I believed it. I have always worked twelve or fourteen hours a day, going back to the time when I was a policeman, and I know it's not a balanced or healthy way to live.

I was also terrified of failing again. As I walked over to St Mary's the day after getting out of hospital, I recalled the voice of one of my friends on the police force saying I was setting a terrible example for the gospel by taking time off after the beating in Pickering. I also heard the voice of the sergeant who called me a "big, fat Jessie" and accused me of losing my bottle. I'd always felt guilty for quitting as a police officer.

Failing God is far worse than failing a police sergeant. I was at the point where I believed that God would be angry if I took time off for being sick. So I thought I had to keep going, to keep ministering for God's kingdom.

A mob of reporters stood outside the door of St Mary's Cloughton. *Shadowmancer* was the number one book on the paperback charts, and it seemed like every newspaper in the country wanted to talk to me.

In the first month alone, more than 80,000 copies of *Shadowmancer* had been sold according to Book Track, making it number one on the paperback chart, pushing Harry Potter from

the top spot. While I sipped coffee and talked to my parishioners after church, Hannah and Abigail were outside, bringing
cups of tea to the reporters.

I had a press assistant from Faber who was coordinating press
interviews, but reporters still came to the church, hoping to get
a quick quote from me or some details to fill out their stories.
During one of those interviews, a reporter asked me what it was
like to beat out J. K. Rowling. All of sudden, it dawned on me
that *Shadowmancer* was "hotter than Potter." A few days later,
that line appeared as a headline in a national newspaper, setting
off a new wave of requests for interviews.

I started to understand that we had to become very careful
around reporters, for we never knew how we might be quoted.
One afternoon I was talking to a reporter in the vicarage office
when Lydia burst in, dancing in circles.

"Daddy, we got the swimming pool!" she cried out. I could
see the look on the reporter's face – the poor vicar was now living in the lap of luxury, with his own private swimming pool.

"She's just talking about a very cheap paddling pool for the
garden," I told the reporter. But even that tidbit of information
made it into an article in the *Guardian*.

Shadowmancer spent fifteen weeks atop the bestseller list
and had sold more than 250,000 copies within three months.
I got a silver platter from Faber that reads, "Shadowmancer,
Number One." It was much too pretentious to display, so we
use it as a dish for peanuts or other snack foods during a party.

Less than a year earlier, we'd been selling copies of *Shadowmancer* from the front room of the vicarage in Cloughton,
and now it was an international publishing sensation. Its success in the United Kingdom brought more publishing contracts
from foreign publishers, including ones for Japan, Poland, Russia, Argentina, Spain, as well as a £300,000 deal from Penguin
Putman to publish the book in America. Faber also signed me
up for three more books. I'd already started work on a new

book called *Wormwood* – not a sequel to *Shadowmancer* but set in the same time period.

In essence I was living two lives; one as Reverend Graham Taylor of St Mary's Church and the other as G. P. Taylor, best-selling author. Soon after *Shadowmancer* came out, the *Times* of London ran a story about my double life, titled "Balance Sheet: Where Does Work End and Life Begin?" It gave a glimpse of my typical day, from the toddlers' groups and RE classes to writing during lunch and all the visiting in the parish.

In the article, the "balance sheet" came out with work at 75 percent and life at 25 percent. But a few things were missing: five Sunday services, baptisms, funerals, weddings, book signings, radio and television appearances and midnight trips to the hospital as both a vicar and a patient. I was trying to cram even more into an already overcrowded life. It was a recipe for disaster.

14

THE MAN IN BLACK

A few months after my midnight ride to the hospital, Kathy and I paid a visit to a doctor friend of mine. After dinner, my friend took a scotch bottle from the cabinet, poured some of the amber liquid into a small glass and brought it over to the table where Kathy and I were sitting.

"Graham, have a drink," said my doctor friend (who shall remain anonymous).

"That's alcohol," I said. "You know I don't drink."

"I'm your doctor," he said. "Drink it."

It had been many years since I'd last had a drink, something I was very proud of. So proud that I became a self-righteous pain, looking down on other people who drank.

"Drink it, Graham," my doctor friend said, "it'll do you good."

My body tensed. What was this about? He might be my doctor, but he was out of bounds here. Kathy looked at me as if to say, "Graham, don't even think about hitting him."

Begrudgingly, I picked up the glass and swallowed it down, feeling the whiskey burn my mouth and throat. Thankfully, I didn't spit out the hard liquor.

"Graham," my friend said, "as your doctor, I recommend that you occasionally have a glass of whiskey. And I want you to have a glass of wine every day. I want you to sit down, and I want you to laugh. And while you are at it, I want you to lose two stone."

Ever since I'd had my first bout of heart trouble, my doctor friend had been after me to slow down. Not only was he my doctor; he was also a neighbour – a very godly Christian with a dry sense of humour. Back in July, he'd concurred with the consultant at the hospital and had written me a doctor's order to take two weeks off. But I'd binned it. Between the church and the book, I had no time to rest. But my friend didn't give up easily. If I wouldn't take a long stretch of time off, then he'd try another route.

"He's right, you know," Kathy added. "You can't keep this pace up."

Even before the heart trouble, Kathy had been on me to slow down. "I think you should stop everything," she had told me in spring of 2003, a few months before the Faber release of *Shadowmancer*. As she was praying and cleaning up, the words "Stop everything" had come into her mind. She felt like God was telling her that I needed to stop before I drove myself into the ground.

But I had told her, "I don't need to slow down." Inside, I was thinking something along the lines of, *I am Superminister, I can do it all.*

Now, even after the heart problems, I wasn't ready to quit. Quitting either the book or the church felt like failing to me. And I certainly wasn't ready for that.

As a vicar, I felt a tremendous responsibility for the spiritual health of my parishioners. People's very souls were placed in my care, so I didn't feel I could just call in sick on a Sunday morning. Imagine showing up to church and seeing a sign on the door: "Sorry, no church today; the vicar's called in sick." In my two years in Cloughton, I'd tried to get someone else to take the services so I could have a weekend off but couldn't find a replacement. So eventually I gave up trying. My fear was that if I stopped, the churches would stop as well.

The danger in being a vicar comes when we become so concerned about everyone else's spiritual health (and their emotional and physical health as well) that we neglect our own. We can become so busy working for Jesus that we have no time to be with Jesus ourselves.

I pride myself on being someone who bases his faith on the Bible. But in this area of life, I was completely ignoring what the Bible teaches about Jesus. What was he doing? He'd go around teaching, preaching, healing people and working miracles, and then he'd go off into the wilderness with the disciples and have a rest. I can almost picture Jesus after the Sermon on the Mount, saying to the disciples, "Right, that's taken care of. Now here's what we're going to do. We're going to go out into the wilderness, we're going to drink some wine, and we're going to have a laugh." And off they'd go.

That's what I was missing. I went to church, I prayed, I read my Bible. I may have been very religious, but little of that was sinking into my life. I ignored the advice of Jesus to bring my heavy burdens to him, and he would give me rest. It's as if I was saying, "No worries, Jesus; I'll carry my own burdens and my parishioners' as well."

It only took a few more months for me to realise how sick I had become. It was a few weeks before Christmas, and I'd come down with a bad chest infection. No matter how hard I coughed, I couldn't clear my lungs. My breath was short and laboured, and I felt like something was gurgling in my lungs. About a month earlier, I'd had to go back to the hospital in the middle of the night with another episode with my heart. I had just started to recover from that when the infection set it.

The coughing fits and the constant feeling that I couldn't catch my breath made for a restless night. Turning my head, I saw the red numbers of the alarm clock glowing in the dark. 6:45. In fifteen minutes, the alarm would sound, announcing the beginning of another Sunday marathon of services. I closed my eyes and tried to catch a few precious minutes of sleep. It had been at least a week since I'd slept through the night uninterrupted.

When the alarm went off, I reached quickly to shut it off before it woke Kathy. The sudden motion brought a wave of stabbing pains through my chest and back. I heaved myself into a sitting position, then slowly rose and walked gingerly to the bathroom to begin getting ready for the eight o'clock service.

I swallowed two large antibiotic pills with a glassful of water. My doctor had prescribed them for my chest infection, but they were not working; the infection was getting worse. The face that stared back at me from the mirror was pale and grey as I washed and brushed my teeth. I made my way back to the bedroom and pulled my trousers on with minimal discomfort. But when I reached up for my clerical shirt, pain shot through my back.

"Kathy," I said. "Are you awake?"

"I'm up," she said, her voice still heavy with sleep.

"Can you help me out here? I can't reach my shirt."

Kathy rolled out of bed and came over to the closet. She looked me over and put a hand on my cold and sweaty forehead.

"Graham, you're not fit to do this service," she said. "You mustn't go."

"If I can just get dressed, I'll be fine," I told her. "I'll rest in between the services."

That was a lie, and Kathy knew it. There was only about forty-five minutes between the end of the eight o'clock service and the beginning of the next service. And after the service, I'd have to stand by the door and greet people, leaving me at most half an hour free. But she also knew that when I set my mind on something, it's futile to try to talk me out of it.

"There's no time for you to really have a rest," she said as she helped me with my shirt. She pulled my sleeves on and buttoned the shirt for me, then helped me with the rest of my clerical garb.

"I'll have a sleep this afternoon," I said, walking out of the bedroom.

In her own way, Kathy is just as stubborn as I am. She suspected that I might have pneumonia or even a collapsed lung and wasn't going to sit around and wait for me to keel over. While the girls ate breakfast and played, she rang the National Health Service call centre. She explained that she was a trained nurse and that she feared her husband might have a collapsed lung. The nurse on the line went through a list of symptoms and then asked if she could talk to me.

Kathy replied, "Well, no. He's a vicar and out doing Sunday services."

The nurse was incredulous. "He can't have a collapsed lung if he's out doing a service," she said.

Kathy replied, "If it's not a collapsed lung, then it's pneumonia. He's so ill that he couldn't even get himself dressed."

The nurse must have believed her, because she put her through to a doctor at Scarborough Hospital. Amazingly, he was a Christian and very understanding. Kathy and the doctor arranged that I could go down to the hospital between services, and he would see me right away. Kathy told me later that he even said he would pray for me.

I got home a bit earlier than expected that Sunday. The service was small, and I was in such pain that I'd cut my sermon short. When I walked in the door, Kathy told me the news about the doctor. So it was back out the door and into the car. While I drove to the hospital, Kathy rang the doctor to tell him I was on the way. In an examining room, he listened to my chest, had me cough and took my temperature.

"You've definitely got bronchitis," he said, when he was done. "I also think that you have pneumonia, and I want to admit you to hospital."

"I'm sorry, but I can't stay," I said. "I've got to do the ten o'clock service. Please, just give me some tablets to help me breathe. I'll take them, and after the service, I'll go straight to bed."

The doctor was a regular guy – in his forties, with dark hair and a hearty grin. "You're mad," he said. "You know that."

"I know," I said, "but I have a service to do."

"And I can't convince you to stay, can I?" he asked.

"No."

"Before you run off," he said, "would you let me pray for you?"

"You might as well," I said. Right there, sitting in the exam room at Scarborough Hospital, the doctor laid hands on me and prayed for me – that God would heal me and protect me, despite my insanity of not being willing to take time off.

As I was walking out the door, he said to me, "Hey Vic – even Jesus took a day off."

It was a salient moment that I will always remember. I knew he was right – Jesus, who was the Son of God, who had supernatural power and had come to save the world – rested on the Sabbath. But even so, I was not willing to quit and deluded myself that if I soldiered on, things would get better.

I shuddered inside when the phone rang in the kitchen. I was shut up in the office at my desk, working on *Wormwood*, and didn't want to be disturbed.

Kathy knocked on the office door. "It's for you, Graham."

"Tell them I'm busy," I said.

"It's about church," she said.

"Tell them I'll ring back later," I said. "Please."

Kathy paused, then I heard her footsteps walking away.

Since the pneumonia incident, I'd become a relative hermit in the vicarage. I emerged for services and my other pastoral duties, but the moment I came home, I closed the office door and refused to come out. Even writing, which had once been a joy and an escape, was now a chore. With *Shadowmancer* a huge success, I felt tremendous pressure to come up with another bestseller in *Wormwood*. My ill health had cast a thick gloom over me.

Indeed, I sunk into a depression, as hard as that is for me to say now. On the outside, I had every reason to be happy. My ministry was thriving: we'd repaired St Hilda's in Ravenscar, St John's Stainton Dale had been reinvigorated by joining up with the Methodists, and St Mary's Cloughton was growing and drawing people to God. I had a beautiful wife and three children whom I adored. To top it off, *Shadowmancer* had opened up a whole new world for us, one in which we didn't have to panic every time the car gave us trouble or worry how we'd get through Christmas. My name and face were on the television and in the national papers. And a book tour in America, including an appearance on the *Today* show, was planned for the spring.

But I couldn't see any of that. My heart condition and the tablets I swallowed to keep it under control sapped all my vitality and strength. I had endured a third episode in November, with my heart racing wildly enough for me to be hospitalised several times. My ill physical health cast a foul mood over me.

I put on a good face when I was out and about. Put me in front of a camera or a crowd at a bookshop, and I became G. P. Taylor, the bestselling author of *Shadowmancer*. Put me in church, and I became Reverend Taylor, the spiritual vicar.

When at home, however, I let my defences down and became Graham Taylor, the sick, depressed and worn-out man.

The only person to whom I admitted being depressed was Kathy. But I tried to swear her to secrecy. "You mustn't talk about it," I said. "Don't tell anybody I am feeling this way. I'm the vicar, I can't be sick."

"Graham, get real," she said. "It doesn't matter if you're the vicar. You're sick. No one will hold that against you. After all, they want you to be well."

One of the people who were most helpful to me during this time was Philip Pullman, my literary nemesis. Sitting at my computer one day and feeling completely overwhelmed at the prospect of trying to write another bestseller, I emailed Philip and J. K. Rowling, asking their advice on coping with the pressure of my newfound success. Within twenty minutes, I had a reply from Philip with his home phone number and a message to ring him. I will always remember that simple act of kindness. I still disagree with Philip Pullman the writer, but I have great respect for Philip Pullman the human being. He is a kind, considerate, moral man who acts more like a Christian, though he does not believe in God, than many Christians I know.

Christmas 2003 brought presents, carols and another midnight run to the hospital. We'd woken early and shared Christmas gifts with the girls and then had a nonstop day of visitors and services. In the evening, we went out to see some friends from the village. Around 10:00 p.m., I lay down, anticipating a peaceful night's sleep and a few days off during the New Year holiday.

Just past midnight, the familiar pounding in my heart returned. I could barely breathe. Kathy woke with a start and could tell immediately what was wrong.

"You're going to the hospital, and you are not driving your-self this time," Kathy told me. She called Margaret Bale, one of our parishioners, who is in her seventies but very energetic. Margaret was at the vicarage within minutes of Kathy's call.

The snow crunched underfoot as Kathy and Margaret helped me to the car. It was a clear night and the stars lit up the sky, but even they had lost their power to cheer me. All I could think of was taking one more step and one more breath. Margaret opened the door and went around to the driver's side while Kathy helped me manoeuvre into the passenger seat and buckled me in. I felt helpless and ashamed for needing help with such a simple task.

Pieces of gravel flew up from the driveway as Margaret stepped on her car's accelerator. She raced to the hospital like a twenty-year-old. Then it was into the familiar surroundings of the emergency department at Scarborough Hospital. It's a bad sign when the hospital staff consider you a regular customer.

The nurses had me lie down immediately and began hooking electrodes to my chest to measure my heart rate. It was gallop-ing away at over two hundred beats a minutes again, and every breath I took was painful. The scene was all too familiar; it had been repeated many times in less than three months.

The worst part was being separated from Kathy. While I lay in the hospital bed, she lay in our bed at home, weeping. She wanted to come to the hospital but didn't want Hannah, Abigail and Lydia to wake up in the middle of the night to find both of their parents gone. She felt helpless, knowing from her nurse's training that my condition was critical. For most of the night, she sat awake in bed, praying for me and fearing that, if something didn't change, she would soon be a widow.

By the time she arrived at the hospital the next afternoon, my heart was back in sinus rhythm. Once again, it had gone back to normal just before the doctors were going to shock and restart it.

I told Kathy when she arrived that I was ready to quit. I was worn out and ready to admit that my "smile and act normal" response was killing me. As a police officer, I'd learned how to push my body beyond its limits; I knew that our bodies are far more resilient than we realise and that often we give in too early. Like a marathon runner, I'd been breaking through walls for years. But finally I'd hit one that I could not break through.

When I awoke on the morning of Boxing Day to the sounds of chirping monitors and other hospital apparatus, I realised that what I hoped was a nightmare was reality. Lying in bed and staring up at the ceiling, I started praying, thanking God for how Margaret Bale had come to my rescue. At some point in that prayer, I hit rock bottom. What if Margaret hadn't been home and I'd tried to make it to the hospital on my own? Or if I'd refused to go, telling Kathy I'd be fine? I might have died and never again waken to see my beloved children and wife. After four emergency trips to the hospital, it became clear that I had to stop or I'd soon be dead.

I was released from hospital a few days before the New Year. My first stop, even before going home, was to see my doctor friend. He wrote me a doctor's order for disability leave. With that in hand, I rang the bishop's office and told him my situation. Once that call was over, I lay down in bed and didn't get up again for three days.

Then the bishop came to see me. As we talked and I revealed all the details of my condition, it became clear that my full-time ministry was in jeopardy. He asked for a divulgence of medical records so that the church's medical authority could decide what was best for me. Three months later, I received an official letter in the mail, announcing that my career as a priest would expire on 2 October 2004. I was being retired because of ill health.

Once again, I thought I had failed God. But I had no time to mourn the end of my clerical calling. It was time for me to transform into the "fat and jolly" G. P. Taylor (as Dinitia Smith of the *New York Times* described me).

The limo pulled up outside of the Fox television studios in New York. It was the first day of a whirlwind tour of bookstores and media appearances, and I was being chauffeured to and fro in the back of a Lincoln town car. I had to break one of my cardinal rules on this trip – never to ride in the back of a limo unless I was going to sleep. I'm a Yorkshireman, and people from Yorkshire don't tolerate airs and graces. They keep their feet firmly on the ground. The idea of riding in the back of a limo seemed silly and pretentious to me.

When I'm at home, most of the time I ride with Nigel Stevenson, my old schoolmate who I'd once hung out a third-storey window by his heels. He owns a limousine service in Scarborough and puts up with my idiosyncrasies. And most of the other drivers I've met don't mind the company up front.

In New York, I was travelling with a publicist from Putnam, who was prepping me for each event on the ride in between. Sitting in the front was impractical, so I rode with her in the back. But I refused to let the driver open the door for me.

"It's my job, Mr Taylor," he told me when I objected.

"I'm perfectly capable of opening the door for myself," I said.

As soon as the limo stopped in front of Fox Studios, I grabbed the handle and swung the door open. Immediately, something almost struck the door and I was shoved back in the town car. A bicyclist was passing the car just as I opened the door.

Thankfully, the cyclist and his bike were fine. The driver put his arm on my shoulder. "Mr Taylor," he said, "that is why I open the door." From then on, he gave the all clear at each stop before I dared to touch the door handle.

At the end of the first day, the driver dropped me off at a massive, gleaming hotel in downtown New York. Still jet-lagged, all I wanted to do was crawl into a comfortable bed. After I checked in, a bellman escorted me to my room. When he pressed the button for the fortieth floor, I knew I was in trouble.

The room, if you can call it that, was larger than the first floor of the vicarage back in Cloughton. Along with a massive bed were couches, a bar, a table, an enormous television and floor-to-ceiling windows looking out over the city. A fruit bas-ket and champagne had been set on the table. The carpet was so soft that my feet seemed to sink down an inch with every step. The furnishings in the room were so elegant that I felt nervous touching any of them, for fear of breaking something.

I hate heights and nearly had a panic attack when I approached the windows and looked down to see the people on the ground looking like ants. My heart began racing, and I knew I'd never be able to sleep in this room.

Rummaging in my coat pocket, I pulled out my publi-cist's card. Her last words to me were, "Call me if you need anything."

So I rang her and said, "Please move me."

"Graham," she said, "I don't understand. That's the nicest room in the hotel. Is something wrong?" I'm sure she thought I was being a prima donna.

"It's too posh and too high up," I told her. "Can you find me a hotel for normal people?"

After a few more minutes of conversation, the publicist agreed to move me. She found a hotel in Soho and booked me into a normal hotel room with a normal-sized bed. When I got there, I breathed a sign of relief and could finally go to sleep.

None of this is to say that I mind being G. P. Taylor, celebrity author. I like eating in fancy restaurants and riding in nice cars and staying in the best hotels. But I am aware that G. P. Taylor is just a part that I am playing. I love the whole bit: dressing in black, hamming it up in front of an audience, being the writer who lives in a secluded graveyard and searches for the hidden meaning of the universe. But that image is not the real me – Graham Peter Taylor, a middle-aged man who's been happily married for over twenty years, who has three lovely children and whose idea of a good time is watching *Inspector Morse* with my wife and drinking a glass of red wine.

The last stop on my American tour was the 700 Club. Pat Robertson was a gracious host and invited me to preach at his church. Since the programme is broadcast internationally, I knew some of my friends back home could watch it. It was a thrill to know the *Shadowmancer* story was going out all over the world.

We left the church and climbed into the limo, headed from Newport News, Virginia, to Washington DC for my last stop on this tour. From there, it was on to New York for my trip home. Just then my mobile phone rang. It was Kathy, and I could hear panic in her voice. I heard the girls crying in the background.

"Someone tried to break into the house," she said. "We had to call the police – the kids are really scared."

Several weeks earlier, a tramp had come to the vicarage look-ing for food. He had been sleeping rough in the forest along the moor and knew he could find food and help at the vicarage. We'd given him some groceries, and I'd talked with him. He had seemed a decent sort.

While I was gone, he had come back, this time asking for money. When Kathy refused to give him some, he became angry. She told him to leave, and when she shut the door, he began to beat on it, demanding to be let in. He shocked Lydia, who was only six, and Abigail, who was thirteen.

As I heard the story, my blood began to boil. I've always had a very bad temper – it comes from being an ex-cop, a profession in which anger can be a useful tool. But that angry cop sometimes creeps into my daily life, and I've had to keep careful watch on my temper over the years.

"Right," I told Kathy, "I'm going to come back and kill him." One part of me knew that my response was irrational, but I felt so vulnerable and angry because I was five thousand miles away and my kids were under threat. If I had seen the tramp at that moment, I don't know what I would have done.

A few days after my return home, Kathy and I went out for dinner while Hannah watched the other two girls. It was our first time alone together in weeks. The anger over the tramp had begun to fade now that I had seen the girls and Kathy and knew they were all right.

Then on the drive home, I saw him. A tall man with long, straggly hair and ragged clothes, he was standing by the side of the road, waiting to cross. I drove up to him, wound the window down, and motioned to him to come over to the car. He hadn't recognized me and thought he was going to get a handout. The minute he was close enough, the angry cop took over.

"If you ever come back to my house again, I'm going to get you," I said heatedly.

"What do you mean?" he said, still not registering who I was.

"I'm the vicar," I said. "Remember, you came to my house and you scared my kids? Never come near them again!"

"We'll see about that," he said.

That was it. I threw the door open and would have leapt on him, but Kathy grabbed hold with both hands to stop me. When he saw the look on my face, he took off at a dead run.

I pushed Kathy's arm away and put the car into gear. I started chasing him with the car, screaming bloody murder out the window.

"Graham Taylor, you stop the car this instant," Kathy said, a look of fury in her eyes. "You are the vicar – you can't go around beating people up. Stop it at once."

My entire body was shaking with rage. All my anger – about this tramp scaring my children, about my illness, about having to retire, about quitting the police force all those years earlier – had been let loose. Now I was nearly brought to tears.

I collapsed behind the wheel, stunned. "Kathy, what have I done?"

I started to realise the implications of my actions. Now that I'd threatened the tramp, I knew I needed to ask his forgiveness. Over my years of being a Christian, I'd learned to keep the distance between my sin and my confession very short. I knew I had done wrong, and the only way to make it right was to seek out the tramp for his forgiveness.

A few weeks later, I had my chance. I went into Scarborough to get something for Kathy and saw him walking down the street. I pulled over, stepped out of the car and called out to him.

"Hey you," I said. "Wait a moment, I want to talk to you."

When he turned and saw who I was, he took off running.

"Wait, wait, I don't want to hurt you, I want you to forgive me. Please forgive me!"

As I was yelling at him, he was looking over his shoulder and running ever faster. He must have been completely confused: "This psychopath's going to kill me, but first he wants my forgiveness!"

Off he ran into the distance. I've tried to approach him several times since, and every time he sees me, it's always the same: he thinks I am going to beat him up and runs away. For now, I'll have to settle for God's forgiveness.

The clock read 1:00 a.m., but I had no interest in sleeping. I was anxious, irritable, my whole body wound tight and jittering with anxiety. All the excitement from my trip to America had faded, and I was back to reality. Going from working seventy hours a week to not working at all had not made me well. My heart was still giving me trouble, and I'd been back to the hospital for another episode. My depression became even deeper. When I was working, I had an outlet for my anxiety and could take my mind off the depression by focusing on the needs of my parishioners. Now I had no relief from the anxiety and gut-wrenching despair.

I paced back and forth across the front room of the vicarage while the rest of the family slept. I switched the television on for a few minutes, then off, then on again, then off again, unable to sit still more than a few minutes to watch it.

Long-forgotten images from my time as a coroner's officer flashed in my mind, of the suicide victims that I'd fished out of the river or cut down from ropes after they'd hung themselves. I began to envy the lifeless young man I'd once carried from his car out on the moor. At least he was at peace.

The only thing I had to live for was Kathy and the girls. I had failed as a police officer, and now as a vicar. God had saved my life all those years ago, and I had let him down. In the three months since going on leave, I had not stepped inside the walls of a church. The shame and guilt prevented me from even praying.

If I had been thinking clearly, I would have realised that instead of taking away my ministry as a parish priest, God was giving me a wider influence. *Shadowmancer* gave me the ability to speak to people all over the world. Caroline, my agent, was negotiating with Universal Studios for the film rights to *Shadowmancer* as well as with Faber for six more books. But the combination of my physical illness and now my mental illness had robbed me of my capacity for rational thought. All I wanted to do was to crawl down into the bottom of a dark hole and die.

As a distraction, I turned the television back on and flipped through the channels. An interview with the American singer Johnny Cash was playing on one of the stations. I willed myself to walk back to the couch and sit down, hoping to distract my thoughts from the rope in the kitchen.

The gravel-throated country singer described the early days of his career. He had great success, but with it came an addiction to amphetamines and sleeping pills. At his lowest point, in 1967, he drove out to Nickajack Cave along the Tennessee River. He hadn't slept in days and, because of his addictions, had shrivelled down from 200 pounds to less than 160. He wandered into the cave to end his life with a bottle of whiskey and some sleeping pills. In his autobiography, Cash said, "The batteries in my flashlight ran down, the light went out, and I lay down in the darkness to die. I was at the end of the line. I was as far away from God as I ever had been or ever could be."

In the television documentary, Cash said that "often it's when you're in the darkest place that God will find you and speak to you."

As an ex-punk, I'd never cared much for Johnny Cash, but that night in the vicarage, I felt like God was speaking directly to me. Tears began rolling down my face. A dam burst inside of me, and all the anger and fear and despair and sorrow I had kept bottled up started rushing out. I wept for what seemed like hours, until exhaustion overwhelmed me and I collapsed into sleep.

When I awoke the next morning, I went out to the car and drove to a church in Scarborough for an early morning communion service. God met me in the service, and I felt a sense of peace that had been missing for months.

In the weeks that followed, little by little I began to recover hope for the future. Admitting that I was depressed was the first step. The more I talked about it with Kathy and other friends, the more I felt free from it. It was as if I'd been carrying a heavy burden and now had extra hands to help lift the weight. I also began listening to my doctor friend's advice and began drinking a glass of wine every day.

More important was changing some of my theology. I'd developed a twisted view of Christianity that did not allow me to be sick. After ten years as a Christian minister, it finally dawned on me that I could be human and fail and be sick, and God would love me no less. I shudder to think what would have happened if I hadn't learned that lesson. I'd likely be lying beneath the gravestones of St Mary's Church in Cloughton.

Leaving Cloughton was difficult. We had many dear friends and happy memories from our time there. During my worst moments, when I was so ill but refused to quit, I feared that St Mary's would fall apart if I left. But the church has thrived and continued to grow without me. Of all the things I accomplished as vicar, that is what I am most proud of.

EPILOGUE

Hannah, Abigail and Lydia stood by the door as the paramedics strapped me to the gurney and prepared to wheel me out to the ambulance. I had not had a very good April, May or June of 2005 – it seemed we were having ambulances out to the house every night. I tried to reassure the girls as the paramedics rolled me out the door. I'll be all right, don't worry about me," I said. "I'll see you tomorrow, I'll be fine."

After leaving Cloughton, we moved to a four-bedroom house on a housing estate in Scalby. Despite my doctor's best efforts, my heart problems continued. I gave up caffeine, exercised, lost weight, took my heart tablets faithfully, but nothing helped. But if I learned one thing from my heart troubles, it was this: worrying and regret don't help.

For the longest time, when I was first ill, I kicked myself for going to London the night I was first sick. I thought that if I had only stayed overnight or had skipped the whole trip, my life might have been completely different. Those thoughts had driven me into depression, and I had to give them up. My heart condition may well shorten my life, but I can't go back in time and prevent that. Instead, I can make the best of the time I have.

After all, we are all going to die. We are all terminal; it's just a question of when it will happen. For some, death will come a lot sooner than for others. So my philosophy is to get on with my life – not to ignore death, but to get on with life, enjoying it and doing the best I can.

For me, this is where faith comes in. As a Christian, I firmly believe that there is life after death and that I will live forever. What form that will take, I don't know. But I do know that I will be with God, and being with God is the place to be.

I've also been clinging to some wisdom from a book I was assigned in theological college, one of the few books from that time that I actually enjoyed reading. It was called *The Sacrament of the Present Moment* and was written by a French priest in the 1970s. The central idea is this: every moment is sacred. Whether you're driving to work or cleaning the toilets or playing with your kids or making love with your spouse, every moment is holy. The here and now matters most. Not what will happen next week or next year, but what's happening here and now.

Most of us live our lives for next week. We're always planning ahead, thinking about the holidays or the next big project, but we don't focus on what is happening right now. But that's where we find contentment, by being peaceful and being at peace now.

The other side of the sacrament of the present comes in focusing totally on the people we are with and the job at hand. Some people's minds are always somewhere else. You may know someone like this – you ring them on the phone and you can hear them typing away on their email in the background. Or you're with them at a restaurant and their mobile rings and they leap to get it, forgetting that they're in the middle of a conversation with a live human being.

C. S. Lewis once said that next to the blessed sacrament – the body and blood of Jesus that Christians receive in communion – the most sacred thing in the world is the person standing right in front of us. Since I've been ill, I've realised the truth of that. When I was lying on a hospital bed, sure that I was going to die, my greatest fear was leaving behind Kathy, Hannah, Abigail and Lydia. I didn't fret much about anything else – about the books or my ministry or the *Shadowmancer* movie. The only thing that mattered was the people I love. In that way, being ill has been a gift, as it has taught me what really matters in life.

During my last trip to the hospital, in June 2005, I began praying, asking God for help. "Lord, what is killing me?" I asked.

The word "food" popped in my head.

"If it's food, God," I prayed, "then you'll have to tell me what it is." And the names of all these foods came in my head – bread, wine, garlic, olives, sugar, fruit – things like that.

I thought it was rubbish, just complete rubbish. Surely my condition was causing me to hallucinate. But I was desperate enough to give anything a try. I knew I sounded ridiculous but asked my doctor if I could have a blood test for food allergies. The National Health Service isn't in the business of doing tests based on prayers, so I had it done privately.

The results were unbelievable. All the foods I heard in my head that day came back as allergens. My nutritionalist did more tests and diagnosed me with a "leaky gut." As a result of my pneumonia and other infections, some fungi have burrowed through my intestinal walls and allowed undigested food to leak into my bloodstream. That leakage causes a surge in adrenaline, which then sets my heart off.

My nutritionalist put me on a bland diet: no wine, no yeast, no bread, no sugar of any kind, no fruit, no garlic, no olives, no tomato sauce, no vinegar. For a year, all I can eat is brown rice, red meat and chicken. I don't know what the future holds. But for today, for this present moment, I have hope. And that is enough for now.

People ask me how I feel about losing my ministry now that I am no longer a parish priest. When I first became ill, that's how I saw it – I was losing my ministry. Now I realise that instead of taking my ministry away, God has expanded it. Because of my books, *Shadowmancer*, *Wormwood* and *Tersias*, I get invited to be on radio and television all the time. Before I wrote *Shadowmancer*, reporters used to see me as the cranky vicar who was upset about vampires and the occult. Now they think I have something legitimate to say and ask me to be a "talking head" on their programmes. So now instead of ministering in a church, I minister out in the world – a world full of people, just like me, who need Jesus.

Life has changed, and I have changed. The creation of *Shadowmancer* has been both a blessing and a curse. And I have to admit that not everything has been for the good. God is still doing a work within me, and I am very much a work in progress. So what makes me different? Nothing. I am just a sinful man who, by the grace of God, has found salvation. I know that having everything in the world doesn't make one happy. For me, happiness is an illusive creature. What I seek is contentment and peace, and in my own way, I have found it. Life can still be as chaotic and disruptive as ever, but through Jesus I have peace.

Am I perfect? No. Better than you? No. More valued in God's sight? No. I am just a child of Adam in need of God's love. I try in my own fallen way to stay as close as I can to God, and every day I fail. I still lie, cheat, murder and fall – every day. I am still bad-tempered, moody and depressed. But God's grace picks me up and helps me try to be the man he created. There is still a long way to go.

Even in the darkest night of the soul, I am enjoying the journey. When I thought I was in control of my life, I was actually making a mess of it. I am just thankful that since I gave my life to God, he has been doing a far better job.

ACKNOWLEDGEMENTS

From Graham

Special thanks to:

Suzan, Paul, Sally, Pete, Rex, Lisa – for food, company and counselling

Mary, Frank and my two sisters – for always bailing me out

Suzie Jenvey – for being a good friend

Mitchell (the Ivy) Everard – for the best advice I have ever had

David Bowie, Mel Gibson, Lloyd George, Matt Watkinson, Philip Pullman, Roman Polanski – for such inspiration

Faber and Faber – for everything

All who work in the media – without you, no one would either know or care who I was ... G. P. who?

From Bob

Graham, Kathy, Hannah, Abigail and Lydia – thanks for entrusting me with your story, and for introducing me to English hospitality and cuisine. Thanks also to Amy Boucher Pye and

Caroline Sheldon for taking this book from concept to reality, to Angela Scheff our editor, to Maryl Darko and Ian Matthews of Zondervan UK for all of your hard work on our behalf and to all the marketing staff at Zondervan. And a special thanks to John Sloan, who first opened the door at Zondervan to me, and to David Anderson of Religion News Service, who first let me write about Graham.

To my family (all the Smietanas, Murphys, Sullivans, Rounsevilles and Gaulkes), the North Park friends group, my colleagues at the Covenant Companion and my lovely wife Kathy – I couldn't have done this without you.

We want to hear from you. Please send your comments about this book to us in care of zreview@zondervan.com. Thank you.

GRAND RAPIDS, MICHIGAN 49530 USA